PRAISE FOR MAKE A MA

Make a MARK in Life captures timeless principles that help both individuals and organizations in their pursuit of excellence. You'll discover challenging and compelling insights into four parts, Mindset, Action, Repetition, and Knowledge. It's your call to action in improving your effectiveness and success in life.

Foreword by Marshall Goldsmith
Thinkers 50, #1 Executive Coach and Bestselling Author of
Triggers, Mojo, and What Got You Here Won't Get You There

Rajiv is one of the top professional trainers and speakers in the world today. He has over 30 years of experience in sales, corporate strategy, and value chain creation. He is thoroughly qualified and proficient to help you and your people become absolutely excellent, ensuring that your organization is at the top in this very competitive market.

Brian Tracy
Celebrated Motivational Speaker and Bestselling Author of
Eat That Frog, Psychology of Selling, No Excuse, Maximum
Achievement, Author of over 80 books translated into 12 languages

With Make a MARK in Life, Rajiv Sharma has connected four pillars of effectiveness and success: Mindset, Action, Repetition & Knowledge, and using these tools, you can create a roadmap to achieve your goals. It provides the key to unlocking your potential and achieving sustained greatness. I strongly recommend you read this book to achieve all that you are capable of achieving in your life!

John Mattone
Creator of Intelligent Leadership (IL) Executive Coaching Philosophy
John is the author of ten books, including four bestsellers

The book *Make a Mark in Life* is a unique piece of knowledge-sharing, rich & very satisfying. It provides the essential wisdom, expressing with clarity, impeccability, capturing the tenets that help organization & individuals performing at the highest level.

It engages you in excellence, makes you think through the goals & make logical plans, prepares you to do your best & work hard at achieving what you desire. I like the idea of SOP for Well Being! You will have trouble putting this book down!

A must-read!

Ravindra Singhvi,
Group Managing Director/CEO,
Dangote Sugar Refinery Plc

An absolute must-read. I have found that the uniqueness of the MARK Model and its sheer simplicity in the application makes an increasingly personal, compelling, and exciting journey. Rajiv has given a brilliant blueprint through Mindset, Action, Habits, and Knowledge to help an organization succeed in this VUCA world.
This book comes highly recommended.

Funmi Omo
Managing Director, Enterprise Life Insurance, Nigeria
Founder, the Funmi Omo Initiative

'*Make a MARK in Life*' teaches with power, conviction, and feeling. Both the content and the methodology of these principles form a solid foundation to translate your thinking into actions.
As an executive, this book is a significant addition to my leadership toolkit.

Stephen Alangbo
Managing Director, ARM Life

The author has captured his life challenges in writing '*Make a MARK in Life.*' The book helps you create a roadmap for establishing the mindset for success.

This book will help guide you step by step to change your destiny and your life. Most of our minds are very scrambled and not going to any focus. He takes this very simplified way and organizes the mind to work harmoniously using the four disciplines of Mark " Action, Repetition and knowledge."

It is a must-read book for everyone.

Sangeeta Sharma
President, Niwe Academy, Canada, niwe.ca

Make a MARK in Life clearly articulates a very personal quest for effectiveness and success using tested and proven tools: Mindset, Action, Repetition & Knowledge where harnessed properly helps unleash your efficacy, your ability to cause to be!

This is a "must-read" for all Coaches, Mentors, and Leaders.

Usen Ekong Udoh
Director, Dangote Academy,
Dangote Industries Limited

Make a MARK in Life is an enchanting framework that revolves around Mindset, Action, Repetition and Knowledge. We elevate our life to another level when we address these four elements, which help to deepen understanding about life choices, improve performance, and achieve success.

Janet .I. K. Jolaoso FITD
President (2016-2020), NITAD, Board Member, IFTDO and
Chairperson, Committee for Women Empower

Make a MARK in Life

MAKE A MARK IN LIFE

'Make a MARK in Life' is based on the principles of MARK Model. The journal takes you through step-by-step process to Evolve Mindset, Take Desired Actions, Build Habits with Repetitions and Create New Knowledge.

RAJIV SHARMA

MARK Model is a registered trademark.

Make a MARK in Life

DEDICATION

To Mom and Dad,
it's impossible to thank you
adequately for everything you've done,
from loving my sister Jyoti and me
unconditionally to raising us in a stable household,
where you instilled traditional values and taught us
to celebrate and embrace life.
I could not have asked for better role-models.

Make a MARK in Life

CONTENTS

LIST OF DRILLS

Mindset Drills

Action Drills

Repetition Drills

Drill 3.1   – Actions to Repeat
Drill 3.2   – Program for The Focused Mind
Drill 3.3   – Be Greater Than Your Environment
Drill 3.4   – Mantra for Your Excellence
Drill 3.5   – MARK Model TOPS (The One Page Schedule)
Drill 3.6   – Positive Thinking on Autopilot
Drill 3.7   – Steppingstone
Drill 3.8   – Making Repetition Fun
Drill 3.9   – Spaced Repetition Exercise

Knowledge Drills

Drill 4.1   – Five Years Forward Exercise
Drill 4.2   – Mindful Learning
Drill 4.3   – Monetize Your Knowledge
Drill 4.4   – The New Journey
Drill 4.5   – Knowledge Application
Drill 4.6   – Become a Teacher
Drill 4.7   – Review Your Skills
Drill 4.8   – Generating a New Mindset

To get most of this book, attempt the above exercises on the note pad as you enjoy this book. You can download additional resources from www.MARKModel.com/Resources.

FOREWORD

Make a MARK in Life connects the four pillars of effectiveness and overall prosperity: Mindset, Action, Repetition & Knowledge. Rajiv Sharma masterfully provides practical and powerful tools that will take you from concepts to actions so that you can create the life and legacy you want. With exercises throughout the book, you will learn to create a roadmap to achieve your goals.

I've written 42 books and sold over 2.5 million copies, translated into 32 languages. In my long career as a top Executive Coach, author, speaker and teacher, I've learned that while you can never guarantee success through principles, practices or ideas, you can dramatically increase the likelihood of achieving effectiveness and success in your life by using the best practices.

Rajiv Sharma gives timeless principles that will help both individuals and organizations in their pursuit of excellence. You'll discover challenging and compelling insights in the four parts: Mindset, Action, Repetition and Knowledge. It's your call to action in improving your effectiveness and success in life.

In the first part- Mindset, you learn to organize your mind, reprogram your subconscious, and align it with your conscious mind. You learn to shape a flexible intellectual capacity that looks to the future, rather than using past limitations to shape your view of the world. This book gives insights on how you can apply it in our daily living as a pre-requisite for making a difference in this present world.

One of the key aspects of life is continuous learning and working toward our goals and accomplishments. Be it health, spirituality, meditation, or wealth creation, we all have goals for our life we aspire to. Very few achieve what they want and become a role model for others. This book highlights how to develop focus and gives tools and techniques to develop a wealth and abundance mindset.

In the second part – Action, you learn to translate your ideas into actions. With practice, you begin to commit to actions that take you towards your goals. This part teaches you how to stay motivated and committed to taking consistent actions. It contains profound ideas that when you practice daily, you transform the way you think and act.

In the third part – Repetition, you learn to design your life with TOPS (The One Page Summary) which helps you create powerful rituals. The author also gives a STAR methodology to master the techniques of repetition and create healthy habits. This part has various lessons for you to practice and begin your journey to self-mastery.

In the concluding part – Knowledge, you move to a level beyond self-mastery where you can innovate and leave a legacy to contribute to the world positively. You go through seven exciting lessons to establish connections in different domains, innovate and create solutions.

This book outlines the positive actions and steps of self-hypnosis for reprogramming that you can take to shape your subconscious mind and achieve success. It also helps fuel your entire well-being and attain excellent productivity, rooted in your ability to improve your self-renewal mindset in four vital areas of your life: physical, mental, emotional, and spiritual.

It's an absolute must-read!

Enjoy and act on this book.

Marshall Goldsmith
Thinkers 50, #1 Executive Coach and bestselling author of Triggers, Mojo, and What Got You Here Won't Get You There.

ACKNOWLEDGEMENTS

MARK Model is a synergetic framework of many minds. It began in 2013 as I was reviewing success literature as a part of my professional work

I am grateful to many students, clients, and colleagues who have tested this material and have helped improve MARK Model.

The program and the book have gradually evolved over the years and represent a holistic, integrated approach from mindset to actions, creating powerful habits with repetition techniques and developing higher knowledge.

For the development and production of the book, I feel a deep sense of gratitude:

- To my wife Neelam, for being firm support in living and practicing this model along with me for several years. She is as instrumental to this book as I am. Thank you, dear.

- To my son, Rishabh and daughter, Arushi, for their constant love and insight. They have been my biggest critics, and also my strongest supporters. They have my unconditional love.

- To my team, Mathew, Tracy, Nnaemeka and Paramole for feedback, encouragement and surveys. They worked seamlessly and brought immense value to the publication.

- To all our valuable clients who have supported Neuro-Linguistic Programming, to build excellence and performance in their teams.

- To all my coaches, Brian Tracy, Marshal Goldsmith, John Mattone, Srikumar Rao, for constant inspiration. Your guidance has made this book possible.

MINDSET

"Believe in yourself and set things in motion towards your goals" ~ Rajiv Sharma

1.1 INTRODUCTION TO MINDSET

"We cannot solve our problems with the same thinking we used when we created them." Albert Einstein.

Have you ever thought about what makes you unique?

A couple of years ago, my family had gathered for New Year's Eve. As we were having fun together catching up and cracking jokes, our discussions varied on different topics and resulted in arguments ranging from light to the loaded. While observing everyone, I began to think, 'Though we are all family, I wonder how different we are.'

We collect a lot of information from the big, wide world out there using our five senses, interpret it further based on our beliefs, values and make it our own. We don't even realize that we are doing this subconsciously.

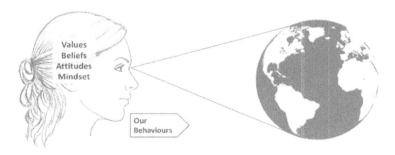

Fig. 1.1

Based on the way we see the world, we set filters, attitudes, and beliefs. We develop a mindset that determines how we will respond to situations and people around us.

Mindset is the present habits of the mind based on our past experiences. It is also an intricate mental map of the world that we construct in our minds. It determines how we think and respond to varying situations, and sifts everything we see, listen, feel, or experience through a set of beliefs, attitudes, and mental states.

Everyone has a distinct view of the world that makes up the mindset. These distinct views stem from our internal mental maps and the models that we have developed through our way of looking at things.

Our mindset determines how we approach other people or situations, and in turn, affects the response we receive from them at a particular time. So, it's our mindset that is responsible for the results we have been getting in life.

Think about this; sometimes, in our minds, we host a multitude of ideas and narratives like 'I'm good at something,' 'I'm not good with that thing', or 'I don't cope well with change.' Such thoughts reflect on the conventional mindset and our fundamental beliefs of whether certain qualities such as intelligence and aptitude are fixed or variable. However, such ideas do not exist in seclusion. They are shaped by our environment, educational backgrounds, and experiences.

Carol S. Dweck, in her book, Mindset: The New Psychology of Success, presented a profound concept of "Fixed Mindset and Growth Mindset" and emphasized the importance of understanding these two facets of Mindset and knowing which one you possess.

Before proceeding, let's first understand how different these mindsets are and how they work.

A fixed mindset perceives our character, intelligence, and creative abilities as innate and static, and believes that we can't change them in a significant way. Further, this mindset assumes that success is the consequence of inborn talents.

For example, some people think that they can't develop their physical muscles, and they create an array of excuses like, 'I have always been like this; I have health problems, or I have no time to exercise.'

People with a fixed mindset continually find faults in their environment much too often and see these faults as the root of their problems. They blame their company, managers, or colleagues; in essence, they look for scapegoats to shield themselves. Rather than facing the fact that they are probably the sole source of their challenges, they present themselves as innocent victims of circumstances.

On the other hand, the Growth Mindset is based on a strong belief and conviction that you cultivate essential qualities through conscious, persistent, and well-coordinated efforts. People with a growth mindset believe that they are individually responsible for developing and strengthening their abilities through commitment and hard work.

Such people have the determination to find a solution to their problem and consciously devote time to develop themselves into the person they want to be instead of wasting their time on trivial things.

They are relentless in developing themselves and are regularly, carefully monitoring their behaviour and words. They look for occasions to add value to other people and create altruistic, win-win situations.

At their workplace, they focus on aligning themselves with the company's vision and understanding leaders' perspectives since they believe they too will lead someday.

A growth mindset spurs increased efforts and
lead to exceptional achievements.

When facing a problem such as looking for a new job, people with a growth mindset show greater resilience than those with a fixed mindset. They are ready to learn and improve with persistent practice, whereas people with a fixed mindset think they are already good at a given task and disregard their incompetence or lack of skills altogether.

Suppose they face rejection in a job interview, the people with a fixed mindset make a barrage of excuses like, 'My interviewer was not nice. He was asking me irrelevant questions. I should have gotten the job instead of someone else.'

On the contrary, people with a growth mindset take rejection with optimism and view it as a valuable feedback. Their thinking process reflects hope and confidence, like, 'I should prepare better for the questions I could not answer. I should also intensify networking with people who have succeeded in my field to expand my knowledge and understand what they are doing differently.'

How to transition from a fixed mindset to a growth mindset?

First, you need to understand that intelligence is flexible, and effort is vital for self-development and transitioning. Read books, enroll in training programs, attend seminars that conform to your end goal, and take notes during those classes. Prepare detailed and realistic action plans and draw clear roadmaps of where you want to be in a given timeframe.

11

Before you begin your journey to excellence, define the goals you want to achieve on various fronts. These goals can be professional, intellectual, financial, physical, social, or spiritual. Self-development is a continuous process that demands you to have an open mind that is always ready to learn.

If you want to achieve extraordinary results,
get ready to put in extraordinary efforts.

Have a sanguine 'Can-Do' rather than 'I Can't' attitude. Take out lessons from your mistakes and use them to march forth rather than treating them as the beginning of your downfall. Accept challenges by seeing them as energizing and motivating while visualizing the joy and satisfaction you will gain from overcoming them. This way, you will discover the immense power and potential you have and tear through every setback and obstacles on your path.

You may feel that you are looking at things as they are, but your thinking is just a viewpoint because someone else may think differently about the same situation. See different viewpoints as valuable inputs to your progress rather than disparaging rebuttals.

Imagine a team working in a retail store; everyone's view of success is different. For team members, success is closing on time and enjoying a happy evening with family and friends. However, for the manager, success is achieving the month's sales target.

Through this case, we understand that scenario may be the same, but viewpoints differ depending on attitudes, mindsets, the end goal, and understanding of work.

Identify your current Mindset and work towards your ideal and desired Mindset for achieving SMART Goals.

Drill 1.1 – SMART Goals

Your Goals	Current Mindset	Desired Mindset
Health		
Profession		
Relationships		
Intellect		
Spirituality		

Table 1.1

1.2 FROM FARM TO FRAME

Once in a faraway village, a young farmer lived with his old parents, a beautiful wife, and school-going children. His wife looked after the family while he cultivated crops on a leased farm. One year, an anguishing drought swept across the land and left the farmer worried sick that he didn't have enough food for the family.

On seeing that their stored harvest from the previous season was dwindling fast and that soon they would be facing imminent hunger, the farmer's parents advised him to move to the city and find some work. At first, the farmer wallowed in fear of the unknown and doubted the wisdom of leaving his family while still mindful of the dire consequences if he did not take action soon. He eventually moved to the city, though reluctantly.

He was not accustomed to the fast life, crowded streets, and the crazy honking in the city traffic. He found a job in a company, but he complained about his colleagues and superiors and did the job half-heartedly. He was nostalgic and missed his parents, wife, cheerful children and homemade food. He felt frustrated with his new life most of the time and performed poorly in his job. One day he decided that he was tired of trying and returned to the village.

With some apprehension and a volley of thoughts knocking in his mind, the young man got to his village. Upon his arrival, everyone was thrilled to see him, and his children were all over him, shouting, "father, we love you. You are working so hard for the family. When we grow up, we want to be like you. You are the best we could ever ask for!"

That night, the man could not sleep. His children's words kept ringing in his mind, and the warm reception he got at home gave him goosebumps. He couldn't bear the thought of how broken they all would be if he would tell them in the morning that he had left his job. To his children, he was a hero. To his parents and wife, he was their pride.

He remembered the bright future he had always envisioned for his children, the business he wanted to establish, and the comfortable life he wanted for his family.

By morning, he had come to a resolution.

With a renewed vision and blazing vigour, he went back to the city, and after pleading with his former employers, he got his job back. He worked with a strong determination to succeed this time around. He now saw his job from a different perspective, an opportunity to provide a better life for his family. As his viewpoint changed, so did his attitude. He began liking his job, colleagues, and supervisors. He energetically and enthusiastically helped everyone in the workplace.

He soon joined a night school, made new friends, and his mind opened up to new paradigms. He was no longer discouraged by the challenges he was experiencing and looked forward to the immense growth opportunities they presented. At the workplace, people changed how they viewed him previously. His managers began applauding his work and referred to him as a model worker.

That year he won the 'Best Employee of the Year' award. His photo was framed on the staff notice board, and he was promoted with an increment. After a few months, he moved his family into the city and admitted his children into a reputed school. Everything was falling into place, and within a few years, he had the life he had always wished for himself and his family. It all started with a paradigm shift in his thinking and attitude.

This is a true story, and I'm sure you might have witnessed similar tales around you. To some people, such incidents are mere luck, but the secret of being lucky is to respond to people and situations in life with a growth mindset.

Our Greatest Success Lies Within Our Greatest Challenges.

I want to give you a powerful Neuro Linguistic Programming (NLP) technique that will guide and empower you to turn your challenges into opportunities.

This technique is **Reframing**. It entails looking at situations or your beliefs from a different perspective and attaching meaning to them. The meaning you attach to the situation is your frame.

When you learn the skills to change the frame, you develop a new view of looking at things.

Reframing isn't about pretending a condition to be great when it's not. Instead, it's about uncovering what could be underneath, what you could learn by moment or how you can use the state to create a better outcome.

Perspective is a powerful thing. When you can reframe a specific experience or interface, you can often change what happens as a result.

Drill 1.2 – Evolving Mindset

Contemplate and write the answers:

- What kind of Mindset did the young farmer display in the beginning when he moved to the city?

- What was making him uncomfortable?

.

- What was the transformational moment for the young farmer?

- Who triggered the paradigm shift in his Mindset?

Learn Reframing from The Story of Tom Watson

Tom Watson was the chairman and CEO of IBM, the legendary tech giant. One of his employees made an enormous error that cost IBM a whopping amount of 10 million dollars. The employee was asked to meet Watson in his office immediately.

As the employee entered Watson's office, scared and certain that he was terminated already, he said, "I suppose you want my resignation, sir?" Watson looked at him and said, "You can't be serious! We just spent 10 million dollars educating you! You are not going anywhere."

Since then, you can bet that Watson had subtly earned respect, cooperation, and his employees' utmost attention.

This is a perfect example of reframing. The mistake had already incurred a colossal loss, yet Watson chose to see this mistake as an opportunity to reclaim some value from his team member.

The same happened in the farmer's story. The situation didn't change, but his view of the situation did, and his story was never the same again.

The truth is, if you let your mind get stuck, you will never make significant progress with your life.

1.3 POWERFUL STEPS TO REFRAMING

- Become aware of the negative or demotivating thoughts that are creeping into your mind.
- Dismantle your old, self-destructive thought patterns and start identifying new opportunities.
- Adapt to interpretations and perspectives of reality that are more helpful and supportive towards achieving your desired objectives.
- Visualize this new viewpoint in your mind regularly.

Practice these four steps daily, and you will gradually place yourself in a more positive, resourceful, and incredibly transformational state-of-mind.

Reframing helps you to contextualize events and circumstances differently and more favourably. You can reframe situations, people, or relationships by changing the meaning you have attached to them.

I have trained thousands of sales professionals and business leaders to apply reframing on things they hear, see, or observe in their day-to-day environment. For instance, when you see a terrible sales call, reframe it as a reminder of 'How not to be.'

One of the most compelling reframing statements is –

"There is no failure, only feedback."

Drill 1.3 – An Extra Mile

What is the biggest challenge you are facing at the moment?

Use Reframing to see your challenges from 3 different perspectives:

a) Visualize what will happen when you overcome these challenges.

b) How will achieving your goals transform your life, family, and your reputation?

c) List the opportunities you'll miss regarding career growth, fitness, relationships, and wealth if you do not move to a growth mindset.

1.4 ORGANIZE YOUR MIND

There is incredible power in our mind hence the mantra, *'whatever our mind can conceive and believe, we can achieve.'*

Every development that manifested on this planet, good or evil, was first envisioned in our minds, be it an invention, discovery, conflict, or crime.

Every day we have different types of thoughts that we need to organize or discard to be more effective. Some are positive, reassuring, and progressive, whereas others may be negative, distracting, and pessimistic.

When overpowered by thoughts, your mind becomes chaotic. The more you dwell on intrusive thoughts, the chaos gets worse, and the more disorganized you become.

While it is great to have new thoughts and ideas, failure to organize your ideas will most likely get you distracted and steer you further from achieving your desired goal.

For example, you might enjoy driving and want to travel to a specific place, but if you keep changing your direction, you will have very remote chances of reaching your destination.

When you organize your mind appropriately and follow a clear line of thought, you can unify your whole being with one goal and achieve everything you desire.

While I was growing up in a small hill town in the Himalayas, there was a big mango tree in front of our house, and its huge shadow used to scare me out of my wits.

One day, having noted my fear, my mother told me a story of a man who went for a walk in a valley of flowers. He was so immersed in the scenery that, for a moment, he felt like he was in a fairy tale. After a long walk, he was tired and thought, 'Wish I could rest somewhere.' Soon he saw a lush green tree with cool shade and soft green grass under it. He sat down under the tree and fell into a deep, restful sleep.

He woke up later feeling hungry and wished for his favourite food. Miraculously, the food appeared on a plate in front of him, and soon after eating, he felt a ravaging thirst. This time he wished he could drink something, and yet again, a tray full of his favourite drinks appeared right in front of him.

Startled, the man wondered, 'what is happening here? I thought about food, and the food appeared. Thought about drinks, and they appeared. Maybe there are ghosts around?'

As he looked around, he saw shadows and his heart almost stopped with fright. 'Oh, these ghosts will torture me!' he lamented in great fear.

The shadows began haunting and traumatizing him as he screamed in agonizing pain, 'Oh, these ghosts are going to kill me!' No sooner had he said those words than he began to feel stiffness in his chest, and he died *of a* heart attack.

This story taught me a valuable lesson that whatever you believe with a strong feeling becomes your reality. When we see fears, those fears become real; when we see prosperity and goodness around, that becomes our reality.

FEAR we see is just False Evidence Appearing Real. These fears stop us from achieving greatness in life.

Pause! Take a moment to think about the ghosts that are killing your aspirations as you encourage them with your thoughts.

Drill 1.4 – Fear to Peak Performance

Write down the fears (hidden & obvious) that are stopping you from moving forward towards your dreams.

Reframe these Fears into Peak Performance

Questions	Your Answers
Define and notice your feelings as you think of your fears.	
Determine how your fear and feelings are affecting you.	
Reframe the situation and feelings for Peak Performance	

The power in your mind cannot be understated. You can develop the mind to the point where whatever you think and ask for becomes your reality. If you seek empowerment, you must take responsibility.

When you discover such power, you must control and direct your physical, emotional, mental actions and energy entirely in the direction of your desires; failing to do so, you become self-obstructive.

Organize your mind to move from a compulsive state of distraction to a more focused and conscious state.

Have Faith in Yourself and Your Potential

Suppose you want to launch your dream business and start thinking, 'it's not possible to start the venture since I need $100,000 to begin, and I only have $10,000 with me.'

The moment you say, "it's not possible," you create doubts about your desire while, ironically, making a plan for something you want.

This way, you are building a justification for not achieving your dream, and by doing so, you are sabotaging the possibility of achieving your desired result.

Rather than feeling overwhelmed by the obstacles, focus on your business idea, and you can find different ways to raise funds like crowdfunding, angel investors, venture capitals, etc.

What you need to do is organize your mind with the mindset tools and techniques covered in the book and, most importantly, be very clear about what you genuinely want.

Drill 1.5 – Mind, Body & Emotion

Write your SMART Goals (Specific, Measurable, Achievable, Relevant, Timebound)

GOALS	Engage Your Mind, Body, Emotions	
Physical e.g. I want to lose 5 kg in weight in 5 months.	Mind	*Mental images of working out, jogging, etc. exercises* *Watching exercises on YouTube, Reading Workout and Diet Journals*
	Body/Energy	*Go to the gym, Jog, Exercise.* *Take the Proper Diet.* *Engage the body in activities.*
	Emotion	*Feel light. Enjoy a healthy lifestyle, compliments from family and friends.*
Professional	Mind	
	Body/Energy	
	Emotion	
Relationship	Mind	
	Body/Energy	
	Emotion	

Table 1.2

1.5 MYSTERIES OF THE MIND

As we have discussed, Mindset is how you see yourself and what you perceive to be your talents and abilities. How you feel about yourself affects your success in every sphere of life, whether at school, workplace, or home. Your life's current outcomes are products of the Mindset garnered from the mental maps you have created.

Let's now explore the mysteries of the mind that motivate you to become more effective in all spheres of life and get better results.

To begin with, let's understand the fundamentals of the conscious and the subconscious mind.

The conscious mind makes 10% of our entire mind and is right behind our forehead in the Prefrontal Cortex. The remaining 90% of the mind is referred to as the subconscious mind, and we can also refer to it as the educated mind.

Let's talk about the conscious mind first.

The conscious mind is the seed of your Personal Identity and forms the spiritual connection of the person you are. It is exceptionally unique and has astounding creative ability.

Let me give you an example of how this works. Suppose I ask you today what you will be doing next Saturday. In that case, your mind will spiral into a creative thinking vision, summing images, and events together to form timelines and activities for you to engage in for the next Saturday.

The creative part of the conscious mind is essential in life as it moulds you into a better problem solver in all areas of your life. Creativity helps you see things differently and also helps you deal with uncertainty in a better way.

The conscious mind is a positive thinking mind and the centre-stage of your wishes, desires, and aspirations. It mindfully and intentionally commands all the activities that you perform.

As you are reading, become aware and feel the sensation in your left hand as you move it. You just did that with the conscious mind, didn't you? The conscious mind makes you fully aware of what you are doing.

The subconscious mind records programs and forms a habitual, reflex playback of past experiences. For instance, once you have learned how to walk, you don't have to recall how to walk; you just walk when you need to. The same happens when you have learned how to drive well. After learning, you drive almost naturally. It becomes your automatic reflex because the sequences get stored as habits in the subconscious mind.

For the first seven years of life, your conscious mind is not fully developed, and you learn by observing and imitating your family and your community's behaviours.

During this period, you learn and are told by others 'who you are.' You get self-identity.

People that indoctrinate programs into you act as coaches, and they might make or break you. Some families may tell their children, "You're the smartest, most beautiful, and most graceful child to ever come into the world." However, some families may say, "Who do you think you are?" "You don't deserve that!" or, "you can do better than that."

The words people utter to you can be of great advantage or disadvantage if you're under seven because you record what they say precisely and keep it locked in your system.

"Not good enough, not loving, not smart enough, not capable."

These are the critical assessments, and parents usually don't mean to install them into their children for a lifetime. They just want to push you to do better, but you download the programs, stating, "Not deserving, not smart, not lovable."

Sadly, your subconscious mind believes everything without filtering or knowing the difference between what's true and what's not.

All your creative ideas, wishes, goals, and desires such as; "I want to be the best. I want to meet my targets. I want to influence my manager, impress that beautiful girl. I want to have a great relationship" are hosted in your conscious mind.

The mystery of the mind is that only 5% of your life operates from the conscious creative mind. So, only 5% of your cognitive activity uses the conscious mind during the day.

An interesting fact is that the moment you stop thinking about the present moment, the conscious mind stops giving attention, and the subconscious mind takes over. This means that you operate the remaining 95% of the day using the programs from your subconscious mind.

But remember, the fundamental programs in your subconscious mind are not of your own making. You downloaded these programs from what other people say about you or from your immediate environment. Psychologists say that 70% of those installed programs may be negative, disempowering, and self-sabotaging.

Since the subconscious mind is unaware and the conscious mind is not paying attention, you cannot see your attitudes. So, it urges the question, which mind is running the show of your life?

Is it the 5% Conscious Mind – where you have wishes, desires and aspirations, or 95% Subconscious mind - where you have the pre-recorded programs?

Since the subconscious mind is the most active, you create your life from the pre-recorded programs. The danger of this is that if the programs are significantly disempowering, you will have difficulty achieving your goals.

However, the good news is that you have the power to rewrite this subconscious programming by aligning it with the wishes and desires in your conscious1 mind.

Don't just accept the programs you get from other people. The instant you get the programs, rewrite them, especially if they are negative. You need to do this so that your subconscious aligns with your conscious mind.

When you align both the conscious and subconscious minds, they open the doors to prosperity and happiness that you so well deserve.

It is essential that you reprogram your mind continually and install more constructive and empowering habits. But first, you must understand the programs in your subconscious mind before you can change them.

Once you succeed in rewriting them, you inadvertently rewrite the destiny of your life.

Since the conscious mind is remarkably creative, you can download new knowledge into it and learn in various ways, such as reading a self-help book, learning from the internet, or attending a training.

Nevertheless, downloading new knowledge into the conscious mind does not change the program in the subconscious mind.

How can you replace the old, incapacitating programs that are already embedded in your subconscious mind with new ones?

In the next chapter, we will uncover methods for influencing the subconscious mind.

1.6 REPROGRAMMING FOR SUCCESS

Let's learn two highly effective methods that will help you reprogram your subconscious mind. Through these exercises, you will align your conscious and subconscious mind.

The first method is Hypnosis.

Hypnosis is a process that involves inducting trance to allow you to communicate with the subconscious mind.

Here you have a hypnosis exercise to practice when in bed. This exercise will enable your subconscious mind to come to life when your conscious mind goes to sleep.

The second method is Repetition.

You have to repeat what you need to learn over and over again to create a habit and fine-tune it to perfection.

Therefore, if you want to change a habit that you dislike, you have to repetitively and consciously engage in a habit that you desire to develop. For instance, if you feel unhappy and you want to change that, you can say to yourself with conviction, 'I am happy…, I am happy…, I am happy!' and say it repetitively throughout the day.

Repetition will change the initial program, and guess what! One day you'll wake up, and your subconscious mind will have already adjusted to the 'I am happy' program.

In this book, there is a section on repetition as it is one of the most effective ways to create new habits and reprogram your mind.

Before you proceed further, write down one old habit that you want to break and two new habits that you want to install in your subconscious mind.

Drill 1.6 – Old to New Habits

1.	Write down one Old Habit you want to break.	
2.	Write down a New Habit you want to replace the old habit you want to break.	
3.	What will you do regularly to form this new habit?	

Table 1.3

Self-hypnosis for reprogramming your subconscious mind yields great results because your wishes and desires sync with your subconscious mind.

Before we begin, let me give you four fundamental rules of hypnosis.

1. The subconscious mind does not process negative reaffirmations.

By this, I mean, if you say to yourself in the hypnotic state, "I am not stressed. I was never anxious. I am not feeling tense again", your subconscious mind reads this as, "I am anxious, I was stressed, I'm going to feel tense again."

So, ensure whatever suggestion you design for yourself, you state it positively and always suggest to your mind what you want to feel instead of what you don't want to. For example: "I am feeling calm and serene. My body is still and peaceful. I am feeling strong and capable."

2. State your suggestions in the present continuous tense.

Using the present continuous tense will make your statements more effective. For example, avoid phrasing your suggestions like: "I will be more confident." Instead, phrase them in the present continuous tense like "I am becoming more confident," "I am releasing this addiction with ease." "I am losing weight daily."

3. Believe what you say with persuasion.

Your subconscious mind can't be fooled. If you just think, 'From now on, I'll approach my day with optimism and joy,' chances are, you will remain in the same state as before without any improvement.

For effectiveness, say it effortlessly and with enthusiasm and also have faith in your suggestions. This belief will reassure your mind and bring the change you desire.

The higher the conscious effort,
the lesser the subconscious response.

4. Focus on a thing at a time and take the necessary actions.

Prioritize the most important goal if you have multiple goals like losing weight, overcoming your smoking addiction, or desire a promotion. Self-hypnosis will not wave a magical fairy wand and get you everything. You will have to support your autosuggestions with regular and consistent actions.

In the Action section, you will get the tools and techniques to help you turn your thoughts into actions. Similarly, in the Repetition section, you will learn how to use the repetition process to create effective habits with subconscious mind programming.

Here is a template of the self-hypnosis technique for five elements - Health, Wealth, Building Relationships, Becoming Famous, and Spirituality.

Practice each of these elements on a different night to have a better impact and create a paradigm shift for life.

I suggest you use these techniques for the next five nights just before going to bed. Before you start, get comfortable and relaxed.

Based on the following patterns, you are free to create your script for self-hypnosis.

Drill 1.7 – Self Hypnosis

On The First Night

Lie down on the bed and imagine you are in excellent health.

Visualize the exercises that people perform for fitness and superb health.

Imagine you are jogging in a park, on a beach, or even trekking on a mountain.

Visualize yourself performing all the physical activities that are useful in creating optimal fitness.

While still visualizing, let your mind replay these images and allow yourself to drift into a deep trance.

Continue envisaging these fitness and health images as you go to sleep and let them imprint on your subconscious mind.

Once the programming starts in the subconscious mind, your mind will activate neurons that will help you take actions for better transformation all night.

Notes

On The Second Night

Envision wealth and success.

Imagine yourself having unlimited wealth and unlimited income.

Now imagine the things you are doing with that kind of money.

Imagine you are touring the world, in business class, and visiting the favourite places you have always dreamed of visiting.

Imagine you are lodging in the world's best suites in top hotels.

You are enjoying the holidays with your favourite stars and celebrities.

If you value your society the most, imagine making profound, revolutionary contributions.

Imagine adding value to people's lives by opening schools, making donations to hospitals, childcare programs, or nursing homes for seniors.

You have to visualize these images in your mind while allowing yourself to sink in deep, restful sleep.

Let these pictures download from your conscious mind to your subconscious mind.

When this happens, you are now experiencing a profound, hypnotic occurrence.

Notes

On The Third Night

Dedicate this night to build great relationships with your loved ones.

Create pictures in your mind of you smiling and experiencing great pleasure. See your relationships with your loved ones as beautiful and amazing.

Envision your family and friends loving you and saying great things about you. You are enjoying beautiful relationships like you always wanted.

Visualize all your treasured ones around you with bright, lovely smiles and twinkling eyes.

They are celebrating your life, happy for you, and savouring your company.

Continue dreaming all night about the beauty of relationships.

Notes

On The Fourth Night

Imagine that you are famous. You are a recognized expert in your field.

People and companies reach out to you for dates and services. They are ready to pay any amount of money to earn your time and attention. They value your contributions and lean on your every word carefully.

You are a superstar. You have the fame that you always wanted. People are lining up and scrambling to get your autograph, and your fans are taking selfies with you. You are an online sensation.

When you go out, people recognize you. Some want to be seen with you, while others want to spend even a few seconds with you.

World-famous television channels are baying for an interview with you. A famous chat show in your country is playing your interview. TV and Radio personalities are competing to have you as a guest on their shows.

As all these beautiful imaginations are flowing through your mind, ease yourself to sleep.

Notes

On The Fifth Night

Think about Spirituality. Spirituality is the point from where you will transform into the new heights of being.

Just before you fall asleep, imagine that your consciousness is flying high up in the sky, and you mindfully look down at the beautiful mother earth.

You are floating in space, and you can see the silver moon and the golden sun. Imagine that all stars, planets, and the entire universe are pumping energy into you. You can feel yourself being enlightened with the wisdom of the world.

You feel the light and the warmth coming from the sun soothing your skin, and this tremendous energy is entering through your head and spreading slowly in every part of your body. You can feel it spreading through your arms to your legs, feet, and toes.

As the energy fills you up, imagine savouring the beauty of the earth from above. Now think of the most amazing thing you want to do this month, this quarter, and this year.

Imagine something extraordinary. Focus on the things that are going to make your life more meaningful. Think about the contributions you want to make to this world. Imagine that you are positively impacting the mother earth, and the universal powers are converging to help you achieve your goals and desires.

While imagining all these possibilities, allow yourself to go into a deep sleep.

You can read and imagine these hypnosis exercises over and over again. By doing so, you will be igniting and fanning the power of visualization and aligning your subconscious mind with the conscious mind.

To accomplish this, you have to focus on the areas of your life and the things you want to achieve – Health, Wealth, Relationships, Fame, and Spirituality, and connect them with the universe.

You are visualizing all the areas of life and reprogramming your subconscious mind to play at the level of excellence.

When you keep repeating these five exercises every week, you will be amazed at how your visualization improves.

Your belief system becomes healthier and more prosperous, and your mind begins to select the opportunities you have been visualizing week after week. This is the force of the subconscious mind.

When you visualize, you create new neuropathways that help you achieve all the goals you have been dreaming of. This technique is highly effective in reprogramming your mind.

1.7 CAUSE AND EFFECT

For every effect, there is a definite cause, and likewise, for every cause, there is a definite effect.

When you want to wake up early in the morning, you set the alarm that wakes you up. Without the alarm, you would probably continue sleeping. In this case, setting the alarm is the cause that has an effect on you.

> *The Cause is your deliberate action,*
> *and the result you get is the Effect.*

A cause-effect relationship is a relationship whereby one event—the cause, makes the other event happen—the effect.

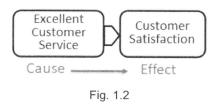

Fig. 1.2

One cause can also trigger several effects.

For example, achieving your monthly business goals will lead to multiple effects.

The first effect is that your performance goes up, and you are eligible for a commission.

The second positive effect is that you gain self-confidence and become motivated to achieve and even surpass the next month's target.

The third effect is that people notice and appreciate your work. These after-effects and continuous performance help you in future promotions.

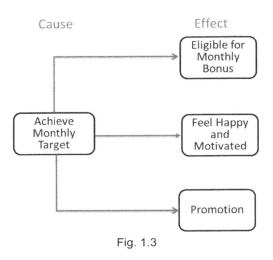

Fig. 1.3

Change your actions, and your life will change.
Transform your thoughts, and you will create a brand-new
destiny.

Let me share with you three fundamental principles of cause and effect:

1. Cause has to occur before the effect.

   This means that you have to achieve your monthly target before you can be eligible for the bonus.

2. Whenever the cause happens, the effect must also occur.

   Similarly, if the cause doesn't happen, the effect doesn't take place. The strength of the cause determines the power of the effect. If you do not have a plan for achieving your goals, your productivity declines, and you feel miserable. Remember, a life without a cause is a life without an effect.

3. A third factor may trigger the cause.

    There is a chain of causes and effects. This suggests that the cause in our example may have been the effect of a different cause, creating a recurring ripple effect.

Excellent service to customers leads to satisfaction. It can help you up-sell more products to your existing clients, which helps you achieve your sales targets, and you are eligible for the monthly bonus, which makes you happy and more confident.

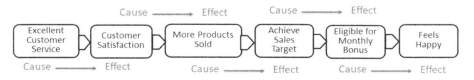

Fig. 1.4

If you make the right decisions and take the right actions, you will undoubtedly achieve the success you envision for your life.

Ralph Waldo Emerson said, "Shallow men believe in luck or circumstances. Strong men believe in cause and effect."

This means that to get your desired results, you must create a mindset that will continuously bear those results.

Think, what kind of Mindset would you like to develop? Is it the cause mindset or the effect mindset?

Knowing the distinction between the two is essential. Many of us live a significant portion of our lives on the effect side, responding to others' whims, desires, or emotional states.

Make a MARK In Life enables you to create the cause mindset with the Proactive Action and the Repetition sections guiding you to live your life on the cause side.

Become mindful of situations and categorize events of your life as the cause or the effect.

Here are three simple steps to help you move to the cause side of life:

1. Be Decisive.

Be fully responsible for the goals you want to achieve.

Everything about you, be it your income, debt, relationships, health, attitude, or behaviour, is of your own doing, not the doing or undoing of others. The person who looks back at you in the mirror is the chief driver of your life. Say, '*Hello!*' to that individual.

Being on the cause side means you have different choices in your life.

Decide to take charge of your life's events and successes and strive not to be at the mercy of how events happen. Commit to taking decisive actions towards your goals now.

2. Be clear about where you are going and why.

The world is full of opportunities, and you need to be absolutely clear about what you want to do in life.

I believe everybody is born with a PURPOSE in life, and this purpose is our cause. You do not find your purpose; your purpose finds you.

Most times, the purpose is unconventional and comes trapped in fears, doubts, and uncertainties.

To fulfil your purpose, understand and act on the principles of the universe and nature and ask yourself these questions:

What is that feeling or thought you could not get out of your mind when you wake up every morning?

- What is that thing that keeps you up at night?
- What are you afraid to do?
- What sets your eyes ablaze with passion?

The answers you get for these questions sets the direction of your purpose. It doesn't have to be precise in the beginning. It can be as general as making the world a better place. Once you identify your purpose, your consistency and passion will guide you into owning it.

The most critical action you need to take is to identify, acknowledge, and honour this purpose. Take time to understand your purpose in the world and then pursue it with passion and commitment.

The main reason why most people don't get what they want is because they are indecisive. They haven't defined their desires in specific and compelling words.

Clarity comes neither easily nor fast. It is born out of feeding emotional energy into the question, 'What do I want to do with my life?' Contemplate this question and think about the answers to see what brings you joy. If your dream is to help people find fulfilment, then volunteer at a senior citizen's home or a vocational school and offer your services.

In fact, doing what appeals to you initially will soon make you realize whether you have a genuine desire for it or whether it was just a passing whim.

You will eventually find something that calls to you so strongly that you enjoy and want to continue doing and will not be discouraged by the setbacks. That is the endeavour to which you must devote more time and emotional energy, and in turn, it will guide you to the awakening that your purpose has found for you.

3. Don't Give Up.

Find new ways if old ones are not getting you the results you want.

If things are not unfolding as you liked, take new actions and explore other possibilities. Above all, you can choose what to do and how to respond to people and events.

Most people get it all wrong by giving up. When things are not happening their way, they move to the 'effect' side and blame others, their manager, circumstances, market conditions, or even their family.

To get back on track, you have to realize that you always have choices in life.

When you are willing to learn and adapt,
there is no such thing as defeat.

There are no unresourceful people, only unresourceful states. Make conscious efforts to stay in the state of cause.

Anytime you feel unsure about what you are doing, pause and take a minute to think about what you want to achieve.

When you are clear about the outcome you want, you understand what you need to take responsibility for, making you more prepared to be on the cause side.

Do what highly successful people do, and sooner than you think, you will get the results they have been getting.

Drill 1.8 – Link Your GOALS to Cause & Effect

What Causes will help you achieve your goals?	Your Goals

1.8 MINDSET OF MINDFULNESS

Mindfulness is the intrinsic human ability that allows us to be completely conscious of our position and actions and not over-react to situations around us.

Mindfulness means keeping a moment-by-moment awareness of our thoughts, feelings, bodily sensations, and the surrounding environment. When we exercise Mindfulness, our thoughts tune into what we're sensing in the present moment.

With every lesson, you move towards a higher level of awareness while learning what you need to do to be more productive and successful.

By now, you are aware that you need to rewrite some programs that are unhelpful and unsupportive of your goals. When these negative programs come into play in your subconscious mind, you need to be aware and mindful.

Your true home is not in the past; neither is it in the future. Your true home is here and now.

Life is only available in the present, and this is our reality. Science has proven that a wandering mind is an unhappy mind. This should give you a solid reason to keep your mind from wandering.

Studies suggest that getting off-task quickly disrupts your productivity; you spend more time on the task, and it becomes harder to complete.

Mindfulness is a powerful technique that puts you in the present, helps you deal with the wandering mind, and explores happiness in every moment of life.

The secret of mindfulness being a source of joy is that when you breathe in and become aware of inhalation, you touch the miracle of being alive.

When you gain familiarity with practicing Mindfulness, you become a better leader, competent manager, superior coach, capable parent, and more insightfully support people who seek to achieve their goals.

Like any talent, mindfulness can be enhanced through regular and purposeful practice.

Mindfulness practice helps loosen the grip of habitual, self-limiting, and 'fixed' ways of thinking and responding to others and ourselves. It improves our well-being physically and mentally.

Here's the exercise to attain Mindfulness:

1. Set aside some time.

   Dedicate time and space to refine your mindfulness skills. Pick a specific place in your home or office and a time when you will practice Mindfulness.

   You can invest 5 to 10 minutes during the day or before going to bed for this exercise.

2. Observe the present moment as it is.

   The aim of Mindfulness is not silencing the mind or attempting to achieve a state of eternal calm. The goal is simple; to pay attention to the present moment without any judgment.

Pay attention to where you are sitting, the room you are in, and the book you are reading.

3. Let your judgments roll by.

   When you notice judgments turning up during your practice, just take a mental note and let these thoughts pass.

4. Return to the present moment and observe as it is.

   While being present, your mind will often get carried away in thoughts. Do not despair. That is why Mindfulness is the routine of restoring, again and again, to the present minute.

5. Be kind to your strolling mind.

   Don't critic yourself for whatever feelings crop up; just practice acknowledging when your mind has wandered off, and bring it back calmly.

Keep performing the above steps, and the results will accumulate.

Now let me give you the necessary steps for the Mindfulness Reflection Exercise; you can also call it Mindfulness Meditation.

Science has proven that Mindfulness help relieves negative stress, improve heart condition, lower blood pressure, reduce chronic pain, improve sleep, and alleviate gastrointestinal difficulties.

Drill 1.9 – Mindset of Mindfulness

This exercise can help you stay in the present and fully participate in what is going on in the present moment.

- Find and sit comfortably in a safe and calming place that makes you stable.

- Let your palms rest on your legs, wherever feels most natural.

- Close your eyes softly, inhaling and exhaling gently, while letting go of all thoughts. During this moment, go within, to that place of inner quiet where you connect deeply to your higher self.

- Let go of all thoughts and begin to observe the inflow and outflow of your breath. Focus on the physical sensation of breathing. With each inhalation and exhalation, feel yourself becoming more relaxed, more comfortable, and more at peace.

- Continue allowing your breath to flow smoothly. Should your attention drift to the sounds in your environment or sensations in the body, bring back your focus by breathing.

- Continue meditating for some time.

- Gradually bring your awareness back to the present moment, to your body while you open your eyes gradually. Take a minute to notice any noise in the environment. Notice your thoughts and emotions and how your body feels right now.

The highest level of mindfulness is creating a "Mindset of Mindfulness"; to be mindful of the things around you.

When you breathe mindfully, it's called Mindful breathing.

When you listen carefully, it's called Mindful listening.

When you drink your tea with awareness, it's called Mindful drinking.

When you walk mindfully, it's called Mindful walking.

When you work mindfully, it's called Mindful working.

The power of your mindfulness and concentration liberates you from fear, anger, and despair and brings you pure joy, true peace, and happiness.

1.9 OVERALL WELLBEING AND FITNESS

Let's understand what fuels great leaders to achieve overall excellence and optimal productivity. They focus on four areas: Mind, Body, Spirit, and Emotions.

Success and Productivity is an outcome of the energy that fuels the production of extraordinary results.

Fuel your energy first. You have to pour in so you can pour out. When you take care of your body, your mind, your emotions, and your soul and align them, you achieve your goals and become delightful and prosperous as well.

I call the proper alignment of these four areas overall wellbeing, and it also includes mental fitness, happiness, beautiful relationships, a sense of meaning, belonging, and purpose.

Your overall well-being is rooted in your ability to conserve and improve your mindset for self-renewal of the four vital pillars of your life, which include:

- Physical Fitness
- Mental Fitness
- Emotional Fitness
- Spiritual Fitness

During my programs, many people wonder and ask me why I use fitness instead of health for these four elements. Well, I use fitness because you work out in the four areas, and the outcome you get is health.

Drill 1.10 – My Overall Fitness

Rate your fitness on a scale of 0 to 10 (0 being the lowest and 10 being the highest).

	Write Your Score
Physical	
Mental	
Emotional	
Spiritual	

In how many areas have you scored a 10?

Most people are generally happy with 7 or 8 because they think getting anything above 5 is OK as long as they are healthy.

It's similar to when you have minor knee pain, but you can walk, nonetheless. You bear with the pain because it is not affecting your walking, and with time, it becomes your way of life. In such a case, you have no problem at all walking, but what happens when someday you are in danger, and you need to run?

Would you still consider the pain in your knee as a minor?

The circumstances in life are bound to change, and you can face a challenge at any time.

Will you be able to face it with average health? Reflect on this.

Physical Fitness

Let me share an experience that challenged me to restart my physical exercises after a long period of dormancy.

A couple of years ago, a CNN headline alarmingly stated, "Sitting will kill you." This topic aroused my interest and made me rethink my lifestyle.

I researched and found that many studies have revealed that inactivity and sitting for long intervals diminish the quality of our life, contribute to chronic diseases, and shorten our lifespan. These findings startled me and initiated the rebirth of my fitness routine.

Our body is unique and incredibly fascinating. We are created to be on the move regularly, and we work BEST when our body is active. It is said that a healthy mind resides in a healthy body; hence we must take good care of our physical health.

Mental Fitness

Mental fitness means having a positive sense of how we feel, think, and act. It also improves our ability to enjoy life.

To enjoy good physical health, we must be in a balanced mental state. We live in a fiercely competitive world and work hard daily amidst challenges to meet our needs and to maintain a decent living standard.

These challenges, though tough, help us to grow to a certain level. However, we are often exposed to a lot of stress that gravely distorts our mental peace, emotional stability and deny ourselves a peaceful time.

You can maintain mental fitness by incorporating mental exercises into the many activities you already perform.

Emotional Fitness

Just like physical fitness depends on a foundation of proper diet and exercise, your emotional fitness depends on a foundation of positive habits and practices. A healthy emotional life is mainly a matter of experiencing and understanding your emotions.

Many people experience chronic stress and feel overwhelmed because they're not very assertive. They find it hard to ask for what they sincerely want and find it equally hard, saying 'No' to the things they don't. Assertiveness is not a communication issue but rather an emotional issue.

Remember, every situation in life is temporary. So, enjoy your life fully. When life presents challenges, draw lessons from the pushbacks and always remember that good days are on the way.

You can also achieve emotional fitness by reframing the prevailing situations.

Here is an example. Whenever anything 'bad' happens to you, seek to identify the lessons embedded in the situation. Explore whether the 'bad' experience can eventually become useful in the future. If it can, are you justified to label it 'bad'?

Suffering begins when you label an event as 'bad' after it has occurred. To avoid distress, why don't you reframe it as 'that's already in the past,' and ask, 'what can I do next?'

An entrepreneur worked hard to win a significant contract but lost to a competitor who used shady methods to get the business. He was jittery for a while, but he soon recovered and moved on.

Eight months later, the client he was pursuing was indicted for fraud, and the entrepreneur's competitor was slapped with a million-dollar lousy debt.

This incident teaches us that you never really know whether whatever happens to you is "good" or "bad." Desist from using these labels and focus on what the next step should be.

Building your emotional health and wellbeing requires regular habits and exercises that strengthen your mental muscles. You can start with lighter exercises and take bigger risks step-by-step.

Spiritual Fitness

Spirituality is the essence of a human being. It is our personal journey to peace and happiness, discovering the meaning of life, and the feeling of connectedness with the higher phenomena like nature, the universe, or God.

This connectedness is not necessarily attached to religion. It can be found in natural surroundings, music, art, or your community. Although spirituality has a different meaning for different people, it is essential that you fuel your energy and align your mind, body, emotions, and spirit.

1.10 MINDSET OF WEALTH

You are the sole determinant of who you are today, where you are, and who and where you will be in the future. Your life today is a summation of your choices, decisions, and actions you have done to date.

These are the three main qualities of wealthy people:

1. They are continuous learners.
2. They have an income plan.
3. They save and invest every month.

Research shows that over 85 percent of wealthy people "devote 40 minutes or more for self-education or self-improvement daily".

Behave like wealthy people by observing, reading, and writing notes. Convert your plan into bite-sized chunks to be able to make workable plans. All self-made millionaires actively plan for their future, create detailed income plans, and take actionable steps towards the life they want.

For example, your goal to earn $100,000 this year might seem daunting until you realize it's only a matter of earning $8,333 each month, $1,923 each week, and you plan how to earn such money.

Self-Made Millionaires don't just save; they invest sensibly as well. People with a mindset of wealth allocate their money carefully and with great deliberation. They know that 'If you take care of the pennies, the pounds will take care of themselves.'

In his bestseller: The Richest Man in Babylon, George Clason explained the key to financial success as 'pay yourself first,' and recommended that you save at least 10 percent of your income upfront before any expenditure for your entire work life.

Imagine the considerable wealth you will create with such a Mindset of consistent saving.

Drill 1.11 – Income & Savings Plan for the next 2 years.

Your Income	Your Savings

1.11 MINDSET OF ABUNDANCE

What does a mindset of abundance mean to you?

To me, a mindset of abundance is believing that there's plenty for everyone. There's plenty of wealth, prestige, and happiness to go around. It also means being optimistic about the future and trusting that things will work out despite the hitches along the way.

To achieve this mindset, focus on the good things in your life that you can genuinely appreciate.

Here is a powerful principle: Whatever you genuinely appreciate and express gratitude for will increase in your life.

Make choices based on the 'Big Picture' rather than a single snapshot. This way, it's easier to balance today and tomorrow. For example, we need to balance development and conservation, or there will be dire consequences to our planet and health.

Focus on the abundance, not the lack. Tune your mind to think there is plenty for everyone in the world.

Appreciate the things and people you have around you. I come from a culture, where before taking meals, we express gratitude to the creator in prayer and the members of the society who worked to put the food on the table. It's important to thank the person who cooked for you as a sign of gratitude and happiness for the nourishment they are providing to your body.

Think positively as there could be great opportunities in great losses.

Surround yourself with people who have a mentality of abundance to get a similar vibe from them. Focus on the values you bring to the business. Network with people without first evaluating how you will benefit from the interaction.

Our life is a boomerang that returns our words and deeds to us, not necessarily from the same person or place.

The mindset of selflessness has benefited many great people. Many great people have helped me rise in life, and I do my part when some people are looking for help.

The universe operates on the principle of balance of giving and receiving.

The more you give, the more you are bound to receive.

From my experience, we do not think of abundance when we are competing for only one prize or one position. The best thing is to give your all and capitalize on your unique proposition and how you can add value no matter the evident limitations.

If you want love in abundance in your life, give it to people in abundance. Envision the future you desire and create the life of your dreams. See it, feel it, believe it, then you will achieve it.

Notes:

ACTION

"Where you stand today is because of your actions
taken so far." ~Rajiv Sharma

2.1 LESSONS FROM THE LEGENDS

"Twenty years from now you will be more disappointed by the things you didn't do than by the ones you did do."

~ H. Jackson Brown Jr.

This quote reminds me of the tale of two Indian cricketers - Sachin Tendulkar and his friend Vinod Kambli.

In a cricket match in February 1988, Sachin Tendulkar and Vinod Kambli shared a record 664-run partnership – where Sachin scored 326 runs, and Kambli scored 349 runs not out. It was a legendary inning that became a part of Indian cricket history.

At that time, it was believed that Kambli had massive potential and would be a star player for the years to come – a future legend of the game - but sadly, his potential was not fulfilled because he wasn't able to keep his focus.

Despite an explosive start to his career, he started to get fouled out on the pitch. He also began to get a reputation off the field – he was known as a party boy, which soon became his lifestyle, while his game was falling on the wayside.

Furthermore, he began to show that he was vulnerable to short balls and not accustomed to the bounce of pitches outside India. Yet, he was unwilling or perhaps unable to put the work in to correct these technical issues.

Ultimately as his performance dipped, he was dropped from the international team. He will go down in Indian cricket history as a player who achieved very little after a promising start despite having the talent.

However, Sachin did not lose focus, and he played cricket for over 24 years at the highest level. The reason for this success can be traced back to his discipline and commitment. He would train every day while receiving instructions from the best coaches around, and he worked tirelessly to improve his knowledge and in-game skill. He also concentrated on the fundamentals of the game and remained humble despite his growing reputation.

If Kambli could have his time again, he may try to rectify these mistakes, but time and tide wait for no man.

There are many stories from sports that teach us profound lessons. You will love another anecdote of two young budding female tennis players of 1990 - Jennifer Capriati and Serena Williams.

Capriati was seemingly a more skilled player than Williams, and that earned her spot in major tournaments and won lots of medals.

Unfortunately, Jennifer could not handle the fame that came with being successful; she lost concentration and direction. She got herself involved with marijuana and shoplifting, which later led to the abrupt end of her career.

On the flip side, Williams was not having it all rosy either and judging by how she was losing different games; it seemed that she needed to improve her game.

The setbacks did not deter her from working harder. When the opportunity presented itself, she became a force to reckon with and emerged as one of the greatest tennis players – hers is an excellent example of when opportunity meets preparedness.

Drill 2.1 – Lessons from Legends

Imagine you had the opportunity to meet young Kambli or Capriati, and you have to give them a piece of advice.

What would you advise them?

Although you may not admit it, there will be some areas of your life where you behave like Kambli or Capriati. You may have talent, but you will not achieve your potential without consistent actions towards your goals.

Life is a journey, and we all are travellers moving from one destination to another. And I am sure by now; you have travelled life up to a certain point. Now look back and reflect on who you are and where you want to go.

You may be a different personality in a different situation. You may do well in a valley of flowers but terrible while climbing mountains or crossing deserts. At times, it requires substantial effort to take action; you may have to make sacrifices.

You need to learn and figure out how to work with your life; your circumstances, feelings, family members, challenges, dreams, and disappointments.

You have to discover 'what' you need to do 'when' you need to do it, and 'how' to do it to the best of your ability. Your life is right here in front of you and waiting for your next move.

Action is the first step towards skill because you develop expertise by taking continuous actions.

"Dreams come true for those who take action on their vision."

2.2 FROM IDEAS TO ACTIONS

In the Mindset section, you have already set your specific goals and the causes that will help you achieve them. Now you need to start working towards your goals.

After setting goals, most people face two situations.

In the first case, people know what needs to be done, but they either don't do it or procrastinate, whereas, in the second case, they can't figure out what to do at all.

In my speaking career, I have seen that people face the first situation frequently.

> Your goal may be to achieve your business objectives, get a promotion, make more money, shed some weight, or just sleep better. You know what you need to do, yet you are not doing it because you're still contemplating what you want to do while researching your options and making plans.

> If your primary problem is that you know what to do, but you're not doing it, then your solution is simple – *Take the Required Action!*

The second situation is a bit trickier.

> Your goal is to create wealth. Should you stay in your current job or leave to search for another?

> You want to get promoted at work, but you just can't figure out how.

> Your business is not going well, and you want to fix the issues.

You want emotional stability. Should you stay in this relationship or stop now before you get too involved?

You want a promising career, should you aim to become an engineer, a doctor, a lawyer, or a sportsperson?

These types of problems can be confusing and leave you stuck in a world of indecision. To address your concerns, ask yourself meaningful questions.

For example, your primary goal is to create wealth:

1. What are the three ethical ways that can help you achieve your goal?

2. What is your number one choice from the ways that you have listed?

3. What have you done about this so far?

4. What do you think you need to do next?

5. What is your commitment on the scale of 0 to 10 to take action on number 4?

Your roadmap to action is ready.

Even if you have several items on your to-do list, you still need to ask the question, "How do I know what needs to be done first?" Because being busy doesn't necessarily mean you're doing what's important, what's needed, or what's meaningful.

Many people keep doing things in the order that life presents them - they live their life by default, not by design.

At the beginning of the year, they make resolutions but do no act on them. And after time has gone by, they regret the missed opportunities.

You will see that one of the most common circumstances you find yourselves in would be "rushing to get a lot of seemingly urgent things done." But while this is happening, the more important or meaningful items are pushed onto the back burner or simply avoided altogether because you are too busy.

You need to stop procrastinating and start taking action. The only solution to your inaction is taking action. It's a skill and a habit, and the more you do it, the better you will get.

But before you begin to take action, you need to know what action to take.

To move from Ideas to Actions, let's attempt the following drills:

Drill 2.2 – Paying Attention to Environment

> Living or working in a cluttered environment can cause stress and low productivity. Organizing your things is a simple way to improve the output and quality of your life.
>
> - Observe your surrounding, become mindful of small things.
> - Look around and find things that need to be organized.
> - Pick up objects and arrange them.
> - Take these actions now.
> - How do you feel after you have accomplished these tasks?

Drill 2.3 – Self-Reflection

- Step back and think about your life and the key relationships that you've had so far.
- What comes to your mind that prompts you to take a particular action to improve your life and relationships?
- If you're not taking positive steps to improve the relationships in your life, then they will slowly deteriorate.

Key Relationships	Name	Actions that will strengthen the relationships
1. Family	1. Spouse 2. Children 3. Parents 4. Extended Family	
2. Work	1. Manager 2. Manager's Manager 3. Team members	
3. Society	1. Friends 2. Neighbours	

Table 2.1

Drill 2.4 – Urgent vs Important

(Urgent vs Important as made famous by the Eisenhower Decision Matrix)

- List the tasks you have been performing. Are they just urgent, or are you actually prioritizing and focusing on the important ones? Are you doing what matters to you? Prepare a list of activities that are truly important but not needed urgently at the moment.

Not Urgent But Important	Urgent and Important
Neither Urgent, Nor Important	Urgent but Not Important

Table 2.2

2.3 YOUR LIFE IS YOUR MAKING – KARMA

*Where you are today is because of the actions
you have taken so far.*

Karma is a Sanskrit word that translates to Action or deed. Just as the law of gravitation is a timeless principle, so is the law of karma. If you take action with positive intention, you get closer to achieving the desired results.

When you work hard and achieve your targets, your work is acknowledged, and you have better prospects.

A young woman was looking for a job. She had applied to many companies; however, she didn't receive a positive response. One evening, as she was returning home from a store, she found a bag near the alley. There were more than ten thousand dollars, along with a passport in the bag. She didn't keep it to herself and reported it at the nearest police station.

After a few days, she received a call from the man whose bag she had reported. He was a senior consultant for a Fortune 500 company. He referred her for an interview at his company. She got the job and was able to earn several times more than she had found in the bag.

*Do what you think is right,
even when no one is watching you.*

"Our life is shaped by our mind; we become what we think. Suffering follows an evil thought as the wheels of a cart follow the oxen that draws it. Our life is shaped by our mind; we become what we think. Joy follows a pure thought like a shadow that never leaves." ~ Gautama Buddha.

2.4 COMMITTING TO ACTIONS

"Giving yourself a purpose adds clarity to all actions and decisions that follow." ~ Marshall Goldsmith

Whatever work you are doing right now, there is definitely a reason it came your way.

I remember meeting Paul in one of our programs for customer service. At the time, he was working as a teller in a bank. He was dissatisfied with the routine work and was looking for something more challenging. He considered his purpose was to impact other people's lives.

One year after the training, he got back to me, stating that the NLP program changed his life. He learned that he could do his work better if he looked at situations from a different perspective. He began helping customers and colleagues with an open mindset. At the same time, he was ready to learn from his seniors how to deal with challenging situations.

Once, he got an opportunity to deliver a lecture in a church. He was persuasive as he spoke from his heart. The Managing Director of a microbank, who happened to be in the audience, was quite impressed with him. At the end of the church service, the MD invited him to his office for a meeting. After a few interview sessions, Paul was offered to lead the customer service team.

Today Paul heads the entire customer experience division of that microbank.

Now, it's your turn to think and reflect.

Drill 2.5 – Connect to Your Purpose

How can you connect your current work to the idea of your purpose?

My current work	My Idea of Purpose	How do your work and purpose connect?
e.g., Bank Teller	Impact other people's life.	Observing, understanding, and helping others to meet their expectations.

Table 2.3

As with many success stories you must have heard of, ideas and actions are conceived by a small group of people or a couple of friends, but only one person or a few pull-through till the end, e.g., Mark Zuckerberg (Facebook), Steve Jobs (Apple). So, you must not just think it and try to do it – you must do it and see it through.

Ideas don't come out completely formed. They only grow to be clear as you work on them. You just have to get started. You can't understand the journey before you begin because things will only become more evident and brighter after you start walking on the path.

So, take the first step, and commit to taking continuous actions.

2.5 DECIDING IS NOT AN ACTION

Let's say that I'm looking at the day and making a list of things I want to do:

1. Decided on the software to use for financial management.
2. Decided to fix my home.
3. Decided to go on vacation to Paris with my family. (They'll love this.)
4. Decided on the type of curtains to use in the living room.
5. Decided to accept the visiting professor assignment for Business School.

Wow! I made a lot of progress today, didn't I? Well, it feels like I did.

Making a decision is not progress, but the resulting Action is.

Don't confuse deciding with taking action. If you observe yourself when you make decisions, you will notice that all you did was Just Sit There.

You might be browsing on the Web or exploring different options, but all this won't be much of an achievement. And—this is critical— The difference in reality before and after the decision is NO DIFFERENCE. Nothing has actually changed.

Some decisions are incredibly vital and involve a reasonable amount of time and thinking. Deciding on a well-planned and enjoyable vacation is essential only if you carry out the plan.

Until we genuinely take constructive action, we can't change the reality of our life or the world around us. All we have done is decide on possible future Action.

It may seem like progress. You may feel that you have attained something, but keep in mind that irrespective of how much thought and energy was used into that decision, we can change it instantly; we can simply think and decide to do some other thing instead.

Above, I made several determinations; however, nothing has changed. You ought to be wary of believing that decision-making is an action that you performed.

Drill 2.6 – Move from Deciding to Action

Your Decisions	Your Actions

2.6 SIMPLY WANTING TO DO IS NOT ENOUGH

I have learned many profound lessons from my parents; I recall a situation from 1990.

It was the time of a protest against the government which required the police to intervene to keep the peace. They were patrolling in the area to maintain law and order.

I was a kind-natured boy, and I got concerned about the policemen and their wellbeing. I told my mom that I want to offer them tea. She is a kind woman, but a straight-talking one too. She replied with customary directness: "Wanting is not enough; you need to do it."

And with that, I took my desire and turned it into action. I offered tea to the group of policemen, which they accepted. I like to think that what I did, played some part in improving the relations between the police and the people.

What gets in a young mind stays there for long. That day I learned an important lesson, 'If you want to do something, do it.'

Many people often think, "I would like to do this or that." We all can think, but it usually ends there. Very few people put their thoughts into practice and take action.

What I learned that day was that action is the only meaningful thing, and nothing changes with just a thought or an idea. Thinking about something doesn't add value. The result is precisely the same as not thinking about it. Doing the task is the only thing that counts.

Reflect now. Are you the type of person who just thinks about doing things and makes resolutions?

I often wonder:

- Why is it that many people think of accomplishing tasks and yet do not achieve them?
- What obstacle prevents people from following through with their intentions and putting their desires into practice?

We grow up getting instructions from our parents, teachers and seniors. We resist and either reluctantly do as we are told or avoid doing it if possible. This habit of resistance becomes subconscious, and we are unable to act immediately, even for the things we deem essential.

We become programmed in such a way that we resist everything that comes in front of us. We lose a great deal this way.

Drill 2.7 – The Habit of Now

The habit of action is the most important thing we must acquire.

- Step 1: Acknowledge your feelings for your goals and your desire to achieve them.
- Step 2: Recall your purpose. Why do you want to do it? Visualize what will happen if you don't.
- Step 3: Do it Now. Start Immediately. Commit to the Action Now.

2.7 DON'T TRY – DO IT.

Remove 'TRY' from your vocabulary. It's preventing you subconsciously from achieving your goals.

"At least I gave it a try."

People use 'Try' to excuse themselves for not putting forth enough effort. It gives a feeling of psychological victory. It's a consolation prize and a way to make us feel better about ourselves. The word 'Try' prevents us from taking ownership of the times we fail.

"I didn't succeed, but I gave it a try." No, my friend, you failed this time. It's that simple and straightforward.

Having trained thousands of people, I have heard many people say, "it was a great learning session, and I will try to implement these great ideas."

I tell them, "Don't try. DO IT."

Remember the Nike slogan: 'Just Do It.' was inspired by a death row inmate's last words. Do what you are supposed to do. 'Trying' implies failure, so leave out this word when taking action towards your goals.

The Stress of Not Getting Things Done

The number one stress creator is not doing a task you have set for yourself or not following through promptly. The stress is compounded when you take on more than you can deliver in the allotted time.

Stress is useful when you use it to your advantage by proactively addressing situations like completing projects on time, meeting business targets, or studying for exams. Stress makes you accountable for your actions. It encourages and inspires us to be proactive.

Accept your feelings (of laziness, boredom, anxiety, or whatever you happen to feel), and know your purpose. Visualize the reality you will create after your actions. DO IT NOW. Commit to the Action immediately.

Your stress will be relieved from the moment you start, and you will go to bed that night, satisfied with what you have accomplished.

Always remember that WE are the creators of Stress in our life.

2.8 THINKING, FEELING AND DOING

Everything that goes on inside you – your internal feelings and thoughts – affects your actions and words.

What you think and imagine about yourself and the world, as well as about people you meet, will 'leak' into your actions.

All achievers have one thing in common: they can maintain a positive state of mind. To put it another way, when they work on something important, they make sure that their ideas, feelings, and body language are aligned, and we in NLP call it 'congruent.'

Have you ever met someone who said all the right things, but you just didn't get the feel of it? Perhaps they were selling or presenting to you. Their message was optimistic because the words were positive, but their actions were saying something else, perhaps due to stress, uncertainty, annoyance, or lack of confidence.

Your actions speak louder than words. I got inspired by Benjamin Bloom's theory of head, heart, and hands in the Taxonomy of Educational Objectives. He cited the three domains of learning in people as Cognitive, Affective and Psychomotor.

In NLP, we call it "Thinking, Feeling and Doing" or "Head, Heart, and Hands." Head is a metaphor for thoughts and ideas; Heart for Love and Emotions; Hands for Action and Body Language.

To act constructively, you need to positively stimulate your emotional state because negative emotions will make you act otherwise. To produce meaningful actions, you need to be in a positive emotional state.

The head, heart, and hands are connected, and they influence one another. There's a quick way to recreate this.

Drill 2.8 – Recreating Positive State

1. Think of the state that would be most useful to you. What do you want to feel? Confident? Alert? Curious? Authoritative? Energized?

2. There has been a time in the past when you felt what you want to feel now. Recall that time.

3. Immerse yourself in the memory. It's about experiencing it as if it were happening to you right now. Imagine yourself there.

4. As you experience the memory, really see what you saw, hear what you heard, feel what you felt. You will begin to notice that your emotional state is changing.

5. As soon as you get the feeling of the other emotional state, your gestures and body language will change. You may walk taller, change your facial expression, or sit straighter.

Re-create a memory of a positive, passionate state and feel it in your mind and body.

Be a great motivator.

The world's best business people are motivators because to reach these heights; you need to be a great reader of people's subconscious wants and needs. There is something about how they talk to you that strikes a chord, hits the right button, and gets you going.

Drill 2.9 – Aligning 3H (Head, Heart, and Hands) for Actions

You need to move between head, heart and hands, which means connecting your logic to your emotions and finally to your actions.

For example, you want to align 3H for promotion at work.

	KRA – Key Result/Responsibility Areas
from -> to	**Your thought processes**
Head to Heart	I am aiming for a promotion so that I can enjoy my growth.
Heart to Hands	I love my work; that's why I am taking actions to achieve my current KRA, to develop a team, and also to learn my next level of responsibilities.
Hands to Head	I am taking actions to achieve my current KRA, to develop a team, and to learn my next level of responsibilities. So, I'm aiming for a promotion.
Hands to Heart	I am taking actions to achieve my current KRA, to develop a team, and to learn my next level of responsibilities so that I enjoy my growth.
Head to Hands	I am aiming for a promotion, so I am taking actions to achieve my KRA, to develop a team, and to learn my next level of responsibilities.
Heart to Head	I love my work, so I am aiming for a promotion.

Table 2.4

For the alignment of head, heart and hands, you can use table 2.4 to connect with the right move in your situation.

Whenever you are working on change or trying to understand people, or when you want to encourage yourself to do something, it can be beneficial to consider all three H's in your analysis and plans.

Establish the emotional connection by engaging your head, heart, and hands and ensure that they are all working together; then, you will be unstoppable, and you will achieve your goals faster than you can imagine.

Drill 2.10 – My 3H Map

Align your primary goal that you want to achieve to 3H.

2.9 MOTIVATION FOR ACTIONS

Action isn't just the result of motivation,
but it's also a cause of it.

Motivation is the number one life skill that everyone needs to have. No one is born with motivation. Every person on this planet is distinctive and has a purpose.

To move towards your purpose continuously, you must be motivated to take actions towards your present goals, which will help your aspirations become a reality.

People who lack motivation always believe, "I will get to that one day" or "I am waiting for the right time."

Motivation is the crucial factor that transforms a good thought into immediate action. Inspiration turns a good idea into a business and can also positively impact the world around you.

Without motivation, you can't accomplish anything. Without motivation, there are no goalposts to target and no reason to strive forwards.

I have seen many people look up to their managers and leaders for motivation. Leaders must motivate their teams; however, when you are aspiring to grow significantly, you need to develop internal resources of motivation. Reduce your dependence on an external source of motivation, as it won't last long.

On your journey to motivation, you need to learn to motivate yourself daily. But before you begin your journey, you need to identify the reasons for your motivation.

Stronger your actions, Stronger will be your motivation.

Drill 2.11 – Source of Motivation

Feeling empowered to achieve your goal is motivation. Answer the following questions to feel empowered towards your goals:

Question	Yes / No
Do you believe that you can achieve the goal you are thinking of?	
Do you have the training, knowledge, and time to do it?	
Do you believe in what you are doing, and are you sure the process will work?	
Is it worth doing?	

If your response to all the above questions is 'Yes,' then write down the primary benefit of achieving your goals.

What will happen if you don't achieve the goal you have decided?

If you have answered 'No' to any of the exercise questions, reconsider your goals and choices. When you perceive your choice, you perceive motivation.

What choices do you have?

Actions for Continuous Motivation

- Join a community of people who will support and motivate you towards your goals, people who will make you think critically. Success is achieved fast when we work in an interdependent way. Take out time to network and build meaningful relationships.

- Develop your skill, retrain yourself. Learn from people around you. Learn from people who are experts and more experienced - no one has achieved it alone.

- Look at the outcome of the actions you are taking. What are the consequences?

- Help someone in need. You will feel instant motivation.

Play the game to win it. Be always motivated, excited, and fill your mind with positive self-talk like 'Let's win the game,' 'We will play our best!', 'I am going to do it.'

Imagine yourself to be a sportsperson. You are motivated by the cheers of the gathering as you enter the field; you want to give them a top-notch game. As soon as you get on the ground, you feel the buzz.

You are in control of your feelings and your actions. You are playing to your highest standard and are not influenced by what the other team is doing. Even if things do not go as desired, you keep your cool, pull yourself together, and continue giving your best.

Regardless of victory or defeat, you keep your head up high and shake hands with the opposite team players. You know that you gave your best and are already geared up for the next game.

Steps to Motivation

1. Clearly state the positive goals that you are working to achieve every single day.
2. Write milestones that tell you how much progress you are making towards your goals.
3. Have a success mindset. You must achieve a task or a goal to feel successful.
4. Develop recognition mechanisms for your achievements. Even small ones. Have people acknowledge your achievements. It may be your manager, colleague, spouse, or friends. Most world records have been made in front of large audiences and cheering crowd.
5. Reward yourself for all milestones that you achieve.

2.10 SOP FOR OVERALL WELLBEING

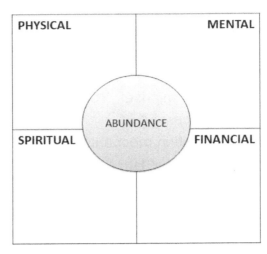

Fig. 2.1

SOPs (Standard Operating Procedures) are also referred to as Modelling Techniques in NLP. Having worked in a corporate environment for many years, I believe in setting the Standard Operating Procedure for life.

Here, I have laid down a standard operating procedure for your overall fitness. We call it ABCD of overall wellbeing.

A- Advocate of Physical Fitness

"Enjoy your body; use it every way you can. Don't be afraid of it, or what other people think of it, it's the greatest instrument you'll ever own." ~ Kurt Vonnegut.

To begin your journey to an active and healthy life, pay attention to the following:

a) Exercise
b) Diet
c) Sleep

Become an 'Advocate of Physical Fitness' in your family and social network. Encourage other people to join as you take steps towards your fitness.

Exercise Regularly

Exercise is vital for fitness, but I have seen people limit themselves to one or two types of activities. For overall fitness, I recommend stretching, aerobics, strengthening, and balance exercises.

Exercise	Benefits
Stretching	Stretching the muscles makes them more flexible and resilient, which increases our range of motion, reduces pain and the risk of injury. As we age, we suffer a loss of flexibility, which prevents the body from functioning well. Aim for a program that allows you to stretch every day or at least three or four times per week.
Aerobics	Aerobic activity speeds up our heart and breathing rate. It gives our lungs and heart a workout and increases endurance. It also helps to burn body fats, lower blood pressure & blood sugar levels, and reduce inflammation. Aim for 150 minutes per week of moderate-intensity activity. Try brisk walking, swimming, jogging, cycling, dancing, or step aerobics.

| Strengthening | Strength exercises build strong muscles and bone structure. Boosting your muscles makes you stronger, assists with weight control and reduces stress & pain in the joints. Develop a routine of bodyweight exercises like squats, push-ups, lunges, and exercises that involve resistance. |
| Balance | Enhancing your balance makes you feel firmer on your feet. It is essential as we get older when the systems that help us maintain balance tend to break down. Typical balance exercises include yoga, standing on one foot or walking heel to toe. |

Table 2.5

Diet Recommendations

A healthy diet is essential for good health. A balanced diet includes a combination of a variety of food. Drinking plenty of water keeps us hydrated and alert.

Eat Daily:	Vegetables, potatoes, fruits, nuts, whole grains, seeds, legumes, bread, herbs, fish, seafood, spices and extra virgin olive oil
Eat Moderately	Cheese, eggs, chicken and yoghurt
Eat Rarely	Red meat

Table 2.6

Sleep Quality and Sleeping Positions

The National Sleep Foundation (NSF) released the key statistics of good sleep quality, as established by a committee of experts. The key factors of sleep quality include:

- Sleeping at least 85 percent of the total time in bed
- Falling asleep in 30 minutes or less
- Waking up not more than once per night
- Being awake for 20 minutes or less after initially falling asleep.

The Minimum recommended sleep hours for adults is 7 to 8 hours. Here are some tips to improve the quality of your sleep.

- Reduce blue light exposure from electronic screens in the evening. Avoid all screens at least two hours before sleeping, including TV, laptops and smartphones. In case you have to work, activate blue light filters.
- Don't consume caffeine late in the evening.
- Reduce abnormal and long naps during the day.
- Keep consistent sleep and wake-up schedule.
- Optimize your bedroom environment by eliminating external light and noise to get better sleep.
- Don't eat any large meals late at night.
- Meditation and relaxation techniques also help improve the quality of sleep.
- Get out of bed if because of any reason, you are not falling asleep.

Sleeping Positions

It is well known how important sleep is to brain health and general wellbeing. Here is a summary of the science of sleeping positions.

1. On the back

Though it is not the most popular position, doctors recommend this as the healthiest option because it allows your head, neck, and spine to rest in a neutral pose. This means that there's no extra pressure on those areas, so you're less likely to experience pain.

2. On the side

This position (when your torso and legs are fairly straight) reduces acid reflux, and since your spine is elongated, it wards off back and neck pain. You're less likely to snore in this posture because it keeps airways open.

3. In the Foetal Position

It is the most popular position for sleeping. It is a loose, foetal position. Lying on the side with the knees tucked into the chest reduces the spine's bending and helps open up the joints. It is especially beneficial for pregnant women.

4. On Your Stomach

Although suitable for easing snoring, this position is bad for almost everything else. You can get back and neck pain because it's hard to maintain your spine in a neutral position. It also puts pressure on your muscles and joints and can lead to unresponsiveness, tingling, aches, and irritated nerves. It's advisable to choose another position, but if you must sleep on your abdomen, try resting your forehead on a pillow—instead of with your head turned to one side.

B- Believe in Mental Fitness

To achieve Mental Fitness, you have to believe in it; only then will you sustain it for a long time. Taking care of your body will automatically take care of your mind.

Exercises for Mental Fitness

- Draw the map of the area where you stay, the route from your home to the office. Notice small things and keep adding these things to your map.

- Start using your non-dominant hand during the day. Sometimes carry out daily activities like brushing teeth with your non-dominant hand. This is because the use of your opposite hand will reinforce neural networks in your brain.

- Socialize and meet new people. Ask questions and listen to them. Understand their perspectives.

- Read books out loud. Speaking and listening to yourself helps the brain to store information.

- Wear earplugs at times during the day. Experience the world without sound! Before you do so, inform your colleagues, family or friends, that you are trying a new technique.

- Clinch your right hand for 90 seconds for memory creation. The same exercise on the left hand improves memory recall.

- Raise your heart rate three times a week for twenty minutes. Practice brisk walking or jogging while checking your heart rate with your smartwatch.

- Walk on the seashore, in the woods, or the park. Enjoy the smell of the fresh rain, pay attention to the birds singing. Your mind will make associations between senses like sights, sounds, and odours that you notice.

- Notice four details in new people you meet. For example, notice the colour of their hair, the type of shoes they wear, or their perfume. We don't observe enough; that is why we often reach a point where we fail to obtain information that our brain should be remembering, but it is possible to cure it. To do so, while sitting in a cafe, pick any one person, and describe them in detail in your head.

- Walk barefoot on the green grass in the morning or evening. Our feet are storehouses of reflexology zones that relate to several organs of our body. By the principles of reflexology, stimulating these points can help relieve the organs' ailments and contribute to good health.

The foot has points for the ears, eyes, nerves of the face, lungs, brain, stomach, spleen, kidneys, and many more parts, so when we stroll on grass, these parts are gently stimulated, and this helps our entire body to stay healthy.

Brain Food

Everything we consume becomes a part of our inner being as well as the outer fabric of our body. The healthier the food we eat, the better our skin will look.

Moreover, the foods have a significant impact on the structure and wellbeing of our brain. The following foods can really help boost our brain function.

Walnut	Blueberries	Broccoli	Eggs
Turmeric	Dark Chocolate	Pumpkin Seeds	Fish
Avocados	Omega 3	Chia Seeds	Vitamins B, C, E

Table 2.7

C- Champion of Financial Success

I am sure you will love to become a champion of financial success because many things in life are linked to your earning capability.

Self-discipline and willpower are imperative for achieving financial fitness. When you are financially fit, you feel good and confident about yourself.

You are in control when you can manage your money to meet your current and future needs. Learn the rules and best practices that others have followed to achieve their financial objectives.

To help with that, here are the rules:

Have Clear Financial Goals

- You need to set specific goals if you want to reach them.
- Plan your expenses and savings to reach your goals.
- Decide how much you would need to save to finance your dreams.
- Always make provision for an emergency requirement in your financial goals.

Understand Cash Outflow

- You need to create a budget, including essential supplies, necessary expenditures, flexible items, and the regular savings required to finance long-term goals.
- Track your expenditure. Check it frequently against your plan and make changes to your expenditure behaviours if required.
- Continually develop knowledge and skills to consume less where possible and save more.

Debt Management

- Reducing debt is critical when trying to enhance savings and asset capitals.
- Prevent high-interest costs and possible fees by curtailing the usage of credit cards.
- Build a debt strategy to decrease and eliminate interest liability. Speed up the payment of loans like a mortgage and student loans if they are a priority.

Put Finances in Autopilot Mode

- Use direct debit to transfer funds to your savings bank account, so you don't spend them.

- Ensure you regularly contribute to retirement and other investing options.
- Use autopay to operate and pay recurring bills like loans or mortgage payments.
- Keep track of all payments and expenditures regularly.

Maintain a Stable Lifestyle

- Do not increase your spending to the same rate as your income grows.
- An increase in revenue, bonuses, and other dividends should be used to boost savings and asset accounts.
- Keeping expenses relatively constant for a long time is a crucial technique in achieving a safe financial future.

Invest Wisely

- Create a globally varied portfolio that will help you attain both short and long-term financial objectives.
- Use a diversified range of global stocks and bonds to get a good return.
- When applicable, think long-term and do not be too focused on the short-term performance of your funds.
- Stick to your investment strategy and review your portfolio occasionally to stay on track.

Learn from Experts

- Being economically fit means recognizing and utilizing the main rules and best methods of saving & investing.
- When required, get help from a certified investment consultant to develop an investment plan and portfolio for your financial needs.

D- Develop Spiritual Connection

During my formative years, I was a keen young schoolboy, untroubled by the burdens of adult life. I recall the day when I was selected to participate in my school's poem recitation competition. I came home with excitement and shared the news with my parents. Together we began to look for a poem that would set me apart from the crowd.

My father helped me select "Abou Ben Adhem."

Abou Ben Adhem By Leigh Hunt

Abou Ben Adhem (may his tribe increase!)

Awoke one night from a deep dream of peace,

And saw, within the moonlight in his room,

Making it rich and like a lily in bloom,

An angel writing in a book of gold:—

Exceeding peace had made Ben Adhem bold,

And to the presence in the room, he said,

"What writest thou?"—The vision raised its head,

And with a look made of all sweet accord,

Answered, "The names of those who love the Lord."

"And is mine one?" said Abou. "Nay, not so,"

Replied the angel. Abou spoke more low,

But cheerly still; and said, "I pray thee, then,

Write me as one that loves his fellow men."

The angel wrote and vanished. The next night

It came again with a great wakening light,

And showed the names whom the love of God had blest,

And lo! Ben Adhem's name led all the rest.

I learned this poem and practiced it regularly. On the day of the competition, I performed very well and won the first prize.

During my school days, I did not understand the poem's meaning, but now I realize it laid the foundation of my spiritual understanding. It reminds me to be humble and kind to other human beings as they are all God's fellows.

An understanding of spirituality may differ from person to person, but the experience of "Absolute Freedom" is the same.

"Oneness" is just one aspect of this, but it is oneness alone that ultimately unites us all as humans beyond the man-made boundaries.

We should help others in need in any possible form.

Helping others brings many advantages:

- You feel good about yourself.
- You connect with another person in some way.
- It improves another person's life.
- It makes the world a better place.
- This goodness you are sending out is going to come back to you.

Make it a habit to do some acts of kindness for others. You can start by doing something small and asking them to pay it forward. In this way, kindness will multiply, and it will bring smiles to many faces.

REPETITION

"Repetition is the mother of learning, the father of action, which makes it the architect of accomplishment." – Zig Ziglar

3.1 LESSONS FROM MARTIAL ARTS

My classmates and I arrived at our first karate class, a bit unsure of what to expect while curious about the upcoming session. Initially, I didn't want to join karate, and whenever my father suggested it, I shrugged.

But when he explained how intense study and practice of martial arts would build not only strength and flexibility but also character, my attitude towards karate class changed.

We charged through the swinging wooden door into the musty locker room, changed out of our casual clothes into our formal martial arts uniform.

I took a deep breath and went into the main hall for practice. The hall itself inspired stillness and respect. Our karate teacher introduced himself and gave a short speech. Quoting Bruce Lee, he said, "I fear not the man who has practiced 10,000 kicks once, but I fear the man who has practiced one kick 10,000 times." And this theme became the reference during all the following lessons.

Throughout the months of consistent practice, there were sessions in which I grew tired, sore, and sometimes frustrated and discouraged.

I remember, in the first month, the love for karate was born deep within me. I was never bored, but one day after repeating a particular move 30 times, I collapsed to the floor, my head down, eyes closed, and was fighting back fresh tears.

I felt too tired to continue because my thighs ached, and my knees felt as if they would give away. I requested my teacher, "I know this move. I have practiced enough."

And in response, he inspired me with a Bruce Lee quote,

"Knowing is not enough; we must apply.
Willing is not enough; we must do."

My friends in the class started cheering, "You can do it!". After hearing that, I kept my mind on the goal of exceeding my personal best as I swallowed and took a deep breath. I lifted my head and looked into the eyes of my strict, patient karate teacher as an angry determination percolated deep within my heart. Rising to my feet, I performed the move with more energy and determination for another 10 times, and it became polished and more powerful.

This process taught me that repetition gives us the opportunity to achieve finesse. With each repetition, I refocused my intention like a laser beam on my goals to succeed. I stayed determined in every class.

I learned many valuable lessons during the karate course. I realized that when someone repeated small steps and the smallest of actions regularly, one might achieve great success. The clearer my mind got, the more determined my resolve became.

With repetition, my muscles did precisely what I wanted them to do. My moves became more efficient, cleaner, crisper, more concise, and more direct. My body almost automatically did what I asked it to do, and my mind was free to be focused and empowered in the moment.

I intensely enjoyed what I was doing, and with repetition, I moved towards control and competence. By the end of the year, I felt like a new 'Me.' I was humbled by the constant repetition yet took pride in practice.

Martial arts inspired me to begin my journey for self-mastery. I learned that I could master any situation, theme, and endeavour in life with guided repetition. When we explore the nature of creativity, the importance of repetition is evident.

Martial arts taught me three significant lessons of my life:

- Repetition helps develop personal rhythms and create mastery. This knowledge saves time and maximizes energy.

- Repetition enhances creativity, increases capacity, and helps develop effective working patterns that result in higher efficiency and habits.

- No matter what the goal is – a work project, getting a new job, promotion, dealing with addiction, a marketing plan, etc., repetition plays a vital role in accomplishing giant tasks through frequent, small actions towards the goal.

Drill 3.1 – Actions to Repeat

List the actions that you will repeat to achieve your goals.	

3.2 PSYCHOLOGY OF REPETITION

In the Mindset section, we learned to operate, correct, and align our thinking with our goals. In the Action section, we came down to acting towards our goals. Now in the Repetition section, we will become the person we want to be. This is the process of thinking, doing, and being.

The guiding principle in the development of repetition is the use of multisensory preparation. The most effective way for us to learn is to engage the Visual, Auditory, Kinesthetic (VAK) to create stronger neuro-pathways. Using VAK produces a multisensory connection to the concepts, develops skills, and with that, we retain new information.

In order to learn effectively, you need to repeat the below actions in different ways:

- See It!
- Hear It!
- Do It!
- Feel It!

Repetition is a key building block for mastery because it deepens your learning on two levels.

On the conscious level, repetition increases your mastery in using the new knowledge and tools you have learned. Increased mastery makes the new tasks automatic, therefore preserving energy and time.

Repetition can be seen as a lubricant for the innovative process, which eases the way for new habits. Have you noticed that when you learn a new skill but don't practice it, the skill begins to fade away? Furthermore, when you return to the same task, some time has to be reinvested in re-learning what you've forgotten. If you aim to maximize your growth, mastery through repetition is very crucial.

On the subconscious level, with enough repetition, the learning on the conscious level deepens and internalizes. Our capacity expands to include reflex and intuition that guide us into more efficient choices and beautiful outcomes. Mysteriously, the subconscious energies become interwoven with the conscious ones and direct us toward our primary and secondary goals more efficiently.

New tasks bring tension by nature because they are unfamiliar. Repetition helps us to grow comfortable with what, at first, feels uncomfortable. This discomfort is an essential ingredient in creative growth. It should not be avoided, as many people do, but rather be wholly embraced. With repetition, discomfort gives way to more comfort.

When we use repetition properly, each action builds more momentum on both the conscious and subconscious levels. We begin to experience less trial and error and more efficient use of our time. This is how goals are achieved, and significant successes are born!

3.3 THE WAY WE ARE PROGRAMMED

According to neuroscience, our mind is organized to remember everything we go through in our life. Our mind keeps a record of our environment and incidents of the past. So, our environment influences our thinking. If you operate by this rationale, then your thinking is controlled by external entities.

Look at your daily routine.

You wake up for the day, and you get out of bed on the same side as you did before; you use the same hand to dismiss the alarm on your smartphone or alarm clock.

You wear slippers precisely the same way, slowly walk into the bathroom, and use the bathroom as you regularly do. Then you prepare yourself for the day. You drink coffee out of your favourite mug or eat the same breakfast. Then you drive to work the same way as you did the day before.

You meet the same group of people who behave similarly every day in your office. Then you finish your work, hurry up and rush home so you can check on your family. You go to bed, get up in the morning, and do the same things all over again.

Pause here for a moment. Think!

Did your mind do anything differently during the day?

We can safely say that we continue taking the same actions, thinking the same thoughts that produce the same experiences, and generate the same emotions, but we secretly expect something to change in our life.

As you meet the same people, go to the same places and do the same things, it is the same external environment that turns on identical circuits in your brain and causes you to think in the same way. As long as you think in the same way that's familiar and known to you, what do you keep creating more of? Same life!

Now, if you continually think in the same way, it's obvious that you will continue to create more of the same thing. You will continue getting the same results, and if you don't prepare yourself for a higher new level, you can even lose what you have.

You need to develop focus and give attention to details.

Drill 3.2 – Program for The Focused Mind

To perform this exercise, sit comfortably. Relax yourself physically and mentally.

As you relax, find a point on the far wall. It can be any point, a spot of paint, colour on the wall, or anything you become aware of.

Now begin to fix your attention on that spot. Do not move your eyes away from it.

You will probably notice that you find yourself wanting to shift your gaze. If you must do so for a moment, you can, but then quickly return your attention to that same spot.

Now take notice of how easy it is to direct your attention to a specific point you have selected and fully immerse yourself in this experience.

Feel yourself being inevitably drawn to that point. Anytime an intrusive thought attempts to come to the forefront of your mind, allow yourself to discard that thought in favour of your focus on that spot.

Make yourself experience that spot.

Notice its shape, colour, texture, and any associations it might have for you. Become a part of that spot. For just a few moments in time, let nothing exist other than that spot.

Now allow yourself to relax and acknowledge your effort in practicing this new skill.

This may seem relatively simple, but this is the nature of the practice. Physical exercises are simple too, but no one questions how well they work.

 If you intentionally practice the technique of directing your concentration to a specific spot, you will develop the skill to automatically direct your attention to those things in your life, which require your attention.

This may be a conscious decision to focus on positive matters to better cope with a difficult situation. It can also be a circumstance where you must focus your attention on a task that you find tedious or unpleasant but still must be completed.

Through regular practice, old habits of subconscious awareness or "default thinking" are replaced with intentionality. And the intention is the essence of focus—the ability to direct your thoughts when and where you want them to go.

3.4 DREAM A NEW REALITY

'Think larger (greater) than your environment and bigger than the incidents of the past.' – If you follow this, it will create your start to true elevation, but if you don't, you will continue to be the same person that you have been so far.

> *"If we do not create and control our environment, our environment creates and controls us." ~ Marshall Goldsmith*

Most people focus on three factors in life: their environment, their bodies, and their time. They not only focus on these three elements; they think according to them.

But to break the habit of being yourself, you have to feel greater than your life situations, be greater than the programs you have stored in your mind, and live in a new line of time.

When you really want to change, what you must have in your thoughts is your idealized self—a model that you can emulate, which is different from, and better than, the "you" that exists today in your particular environment, body, and time.

Every great person in history learned how to do this, and you can attain greatness once you master the concepts and techniques. You can overcome your environment, your body and time. Your mind has the power to do this and also control your environment.

Mahatma Gandhi, Martin Luther King Jr. and Abraham Lincoln, Nelson Mandela, and many other great leaders became greater than their environment with Meditation. Use meditation as a tool and not a means.

Drill 3.3 – Be Greater Than Your Environment

Steps to become greater than your environment:

- Sit down and close your eyes. You need to disconnect yourself from your surroundings. When you see fewer things, less stimulation goes to your brain. When you're playing soft music or having earplugs on, less sensory information goes to your brain, which helps you disconnect from your environment.

- Get to a state where you're not experiencing and feeling anything, think about your future-self and focus on being defined by that thought.

- Become aware as your body goes back to its emotional past. Don't resist; just bring back your attention to what you want to become in the future.

- Every time your body craves old emotions and memories, smile and tell your mind that your will is getting stronger than the programs in your subconscious mind.

- With repetition of this exercise, a time will come when your body will no longer be the mind, and when it finally surrenders, you will feel the liberation of energy.

- Imagine the exact person of your future, describe the details of what you see, hear, and feel.

3.5 KNOWING WHAT TO REPEAT

All great people in history had an idea in their mind; they all had a dream.

Their thought was not in the physical world; other people couldn't feel it, see it, taste it, or hear it. Although their idea was alive only in their thoughts, it was so active in their mind that they began to live as if that was their reality.

Similarly, you can believe in the future that you cannot see or feel with your five senses yet. But you have to think about it so many times in your mind that your mind believes it to be true and look at it like the occasion has happened. Neurosciences say this is possible.

A coach and a leader repeat instructions time and again. The reason they use repetition is that it works. Redoing something many times strengthens the actions, builds a reflex, and eventually gets accepted by the subconscious as being the truth.

Repetition is used as a great marketing tool. Companies advertise their products over and over again on numerous platforms like newspapers, television, display boards, digital media, etc.

You would also have noticed that many political leaders repeat the same messages endlessly no matter what the question is. News media formulate and repeat the same opinions day after day.

Repetition is a powerful and persuasive tool that can be used to align your inner and outer world.

So, repeat your thoughts about the future; what you want to become.

Drill 3.4 - Mantra for Your Personal & Professional Excellence

	Thoughts of Personal Excellence	Actions of Personal Excellence
	Benchmark yourself against the best. Example: Imagine you are working on your • Conversation Capability • Enhancing Vocabulary • Improving Focus	*Find the model person who will be your benchmark and practice to match.* Example: Everyday actions: • Speaking in front of the mirror. • Using new words • Keeping phone notification off
1.		
2.		
3.		
4.		
5.		

3.6 Creating New Habits with TOPS (The One Page Schedule)

Everyone wants to have a fit body, a sound mind and wants to be efficient in their field, but this doesn't happen overnight. You need to program your behaviours with new habits like exercising, eating healthy food, and getting your work done timely.

Let's create a 90-Days schedule for self-discipline. Using repetition during these 90 days, you will create new habits that will develop the person of the future, which you just envisioned. It is going to be an interesting journey that you should log.

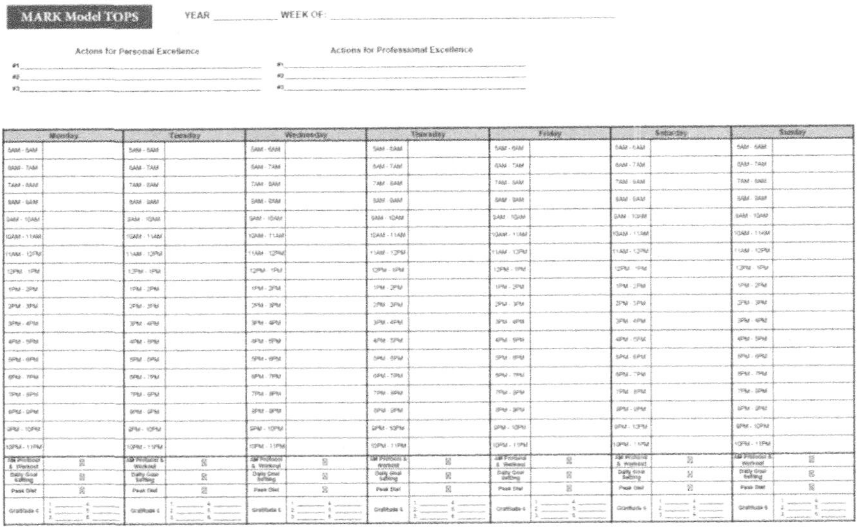

MARK Model TOPS YEAR ________ WEEK OF: ____________________

Actions for Personal Excellence
#1 ____________________
#2 ____________________
#3 ____________________

Actions for Professional Excellence
#1 ____________________
#2 ____________________
#3 ____________________

Monday		Tuesday		Wednesday		Thursday		Friday		Saturday		Sunday	
5AM - 6AM		5AM - 6AM		5AM - 6AM		5AM - 6AM		5AM - 6AM		5AM - 6AM		5AM - 6AM	
6AM - 7AM		6AM - 7AM		6AM - 7AM		6AM - 7AM		6AM - 7AM		6AM - 7AM		6AM - 7AM	
7AM - 8AM		7AM - 8AM		7AM - 8AM		7AM - 8AM		7AM - 8AM		7AM - 8AM		7AM - 8AM	
8AM - 9AM		8AM - 9AM		8AM - 9AM		8AM - 9AM		8AM - 9AM		8AM - 9AM		8AM - 9AM	
9AM - 10AM		9AM - 10AM		9AM - 10AM		9AM - 10AM		9AM - 10AM		9AM - 10AM		9AM - 10AM	
10AM - 11AM		10AM - 11AM		10AM - 11AM		10AM - 11AM		10AM - 11AM		10AM - 11AM		10AM - 11AM	
11AM - 12PM		11AM - 12PM		11AM - 12PM		11AM - 12PM		11AM - 12PM		11AM - 12PM		11AM - 12PM	
12PM - 1PM		12PM - 1PM		12PM - 1PM		12PM - 1PM		12PM - 1PM		12PM - 1PM		12PM - 1PM	
1PM - 2PM		1PM - 2PM		1PM - 2PM		1PM - 2PM		1PM - 2PM		1PM - 2PM		1PM - 2PM	
2PM - 3PM		2PM - 3PM		2PM - 3PM		2PM - 3PM		2PM - 3PM		2PM - 3PM		2PM - 3PM	
3PM - 4PM		3PM - 4PM		3PM - 4PM		3PM - 4PM		3PM - 4PM		3PM - 4PM		3PM - 4PM	
4PM - 5PM		4PM - 5PM		4PM - 5PM		4PM - 5PM		4PM - 5PM		4PM - 5PM		4PM - 5PM	
5PM - 6PM		5PM - 6PM		5PM - 6PM		5PM - 6PM		5PM - 6PM		5PM - 6PM		5PM - 6PM	
6PM - 7PM		6PM - 7PM		6PM - 7PM		6PM - 7PM		6PM - 7PM		6PM - 7PM		6PM - 7PM	
7PM - 8PM		7PM - 8PM		7PM - 8PM		7PM - 8PM		7PM - 8PM		7PM - 8PM		7PM - 8PM	
8PM - 9PM		8PM - 9PM		8PM - 9PM		8PM - 9PM		8PM - 9PM		8PM - 9PM		8PM - 9PM	
9PM - 10PM		9PM - 10PM		9PM - 10PM		9PM - 10PM		9PM - 10PM		9PM - 10PM		9PM - 10PM	
10PM - 11PM		10PM - 11PM		10PM - 11PM		10PM - 11PM		10PM - 11PM		10PM - 11PM		10PM - 11PM	
AM Protocol & Workout	☐	AM Protocol & Workout	☐	AM Protocol & Workout	☐	AM Protocol & Workout	☐	AM Protocol & Workout	☐	AM Protocol & Workout	☐	AM Protocol & Workout	☐
Daily Goal Setting	☐	Daily Goal Setting	☐	Daily Goal Setting	☐	Daily Goal Setting	☐	Daily Goal Setting	☐	Daily Goal Setting	☐	Daily Goal Setting	☐
Peak Diet	☐	Peak Diet	☐	Peak Diet	☐	Peak Diet	☐	Peak Diet	☐	Peak Diet	☐	Peak Diet	☐
Gratitude 6	1. 2. 3. 4. 5. 6.	Gratitude 6	1. 2. 3. 4. 5. 6.	Gratitude 6	1. 2. 3. 4. 5. 6.	Gratitude 6	1. 2. 3. 4. 5. 6.	Gratitude 6	1. 2. 3. 4. 5. 6.	Gratitude 6	1. 2. 3. 4. 5. 6.	Gratitude 6	1. 2. 3. 4. 5. 6.

Fig. 3.1

Drill 3.5 - MARK Model TOPS (The One Page Schedule)

Please visit www.MARKModel.com/resources/ to download and print TOPS.

Write your schedules to accommodate the action for the goals you want to achieve.

3.7 STAR REPETITION FOR BUILDING HABITS

You are the product of your habits. If you want to enhance your effectiveness, all you need is new habits. If you do what you have always done, you will get the same results you have always gotten.

In the book 'The Power of Habit,' the author Charles Duhigg explains that we build habits over time by making a loop that we repeat over and over again. It's that cycle that reinforces habits in our minds. He gave a three-step process that creates every habit:

- Cue
- Routine
- Reward

In basic terms, here's how it works:

A habit is created when a cue signals a routine that rewards the brain. When that feedback loop is generated, your brain doesn't question the decisions about that loop.

We devote most of our time understanding cues that predict rewards like power and status, money and fame, love and friendship, praise and approval, or a sense of our satisfaction. These pursuits also ultimately enhance our odds of survival and reproduction, which is the deeper purpose behind everything we do.

Repetition STAR is a four-step pattern of every habit, and your brain runs through these steps in the same order each time you want to create a habit.

Repetition STAR

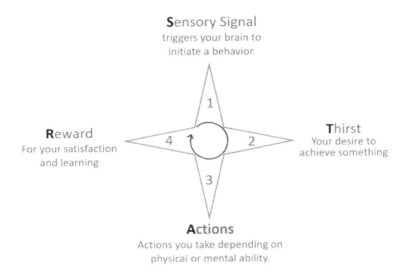

Sensory Signal
triggers your brain to
initiate a behavior.

Reward
For your satisfaction
and learning

Thirst
Your desire to
achieve something

Actions
Actions you take depending on
physical or mental ability.

Fig. 3.2

Step 1:

When we see a reward that appeals to us, a sensory signal triggers our brain to initiate that behaviour.

Our mind is continuously analysing our internal and external environment for hints of where rewards are located. This signal is the first indication that we're close to a reward; it naturally leads to a desire for that reward. Here is a question,

What rewards are you looking for in the next 12 months?

Step 2:

Now we are thirsty (hungry) to get this award. These are the motivational forces behind every habit. Without some level of motivation or desire, without craving a change; we have no reason to act.

Remember, what you crave is not the habit itself but the change in state it delivers. You do not crave drinking tea; you crave the feeling of relief it provides. You do not covet taking a bath but rather the feeling of a clean body. You do not want to watch Netflix; you want entertainment. Every craving is related to a desire to alter your internal state. Food for thought,

Why do you desire these rewards?

Step3:

Your action to your thirst is the actual habit you perform. Whether you take action or not, depends on how determined you are and how much tension is coupled with the behaviour.

If a specific action entails more physical or mental effort than you are willing to expend, then you may not do it.

Your action also depends on your capability. That is, an action can occur only if you are competent in doing it.

For example, a person needs to study medicine and have adequate experience before treating patients.

What consistent actions will you take to achieve the desired rewards?

Step 4:

When we take the required action consistently towards the desired goal, we get the desired reward. Rewards are the end objective of every habit.

The STAR Repetition begins with a sensory signal that notices the reward we desire. The thirst is about wanting the reward, while the answer is about obtaining the reward.

We chase rewards to feel gratification. Rewards offer their benefits; however, the primary reason we want to achieve them is for our fulfilment.

Water and food provide the energy we need to stay alive. Getting a promotion at work brings more income and respect. Getting in shape improves our fitness and socializing prospects. But the more instant benefit attaining these rewards is to satisfy our craving to eat or gain status or improve health. For the short term, rewards deliver contentment and relief from craving.

Rewards provide life lessons to us by teaching us which actions are worth remembering in the future, and our brain is a reward detector. As we go about our life, our sensory nervous system is continuously monitoring which actions satisfy our needs and bring pleasure.

Feelings of joy and distress are part of the feedback system that helps our brain differentiate useful actions from worthless ones.

Getting a reward closes the desire-loop and completes the repetition cycle.

Repeat these four steps deliberately to create new habits, and they will become your behaviour.

"Depending on what they are,
our habits will either make us or break us.
We become what we repeatedly do."
~ Sean Covey

3.8 POSITIVE THINKING ON AUTOPILOT

Positive affirmations are phrases that you repeat regularly, which describe a specific outcome or who you want to be.

The power of affirmations is in their repetition. Slowly but surely, the affirmations sink into the background of your mind, and your subconscious mind can and will hear them. At first, these affirmations might not be true, but with constant repetition, your subconscious mind will start to believe them.

When you repeat the basics, you not only become great; you will stay great. It's a challenge that all high performers face. I repeat the basics of many things in my life: Fitness, philosophy, kindness, business, writing, coaching. For example, I re-read my favourite books to exercise my mind.

Affirmations, auto-suggestions are the most important key steps in the journey to success. E.g., you can tell yourself repeatedly, "I am in a state of fulfilment, I have abundant love and joy in my life, and I am free to do whatever I wish to do."

You rewire your brain by Reading, Writing, Listening, Saying (Self-Talk), Doing and Watching. The people you hang out with also affect your thinking patterns.

If you convince your subconscious mind that you believe you will receive what you ask, it will act upon that belief. Make definite plans for achieving what you desire.

Drill 3.6 – Positive Thinking on Autopilot

List affirmations that you will repeat:

"Any impulse of thought which is repeatedly passed on to the subconscious mind is finally accepted and acted upon by the subconscious mind, which proceeds to translate that impulse into its physical equivalent by the most practical procedure available" — Napoleon Hill

All thoughts which have been given feelings begin immediately to translate themselves into their physical counterpart.

Many people accept they are shackled to poverty and failure because of their ill fate over which they believe they have no control. They create their misfortunes because of these negative beliefs picked up by the subconscious mind and are brought to reality.

Pass any desire that you wish to manifest into its physical or monetary equivalent to your subconscious mind, believing it will come true.

You can overcome big problems by using repetition, doing a thing over and over again until you reach a point where you have subconscious competence.

E.g., when you are driving, you automatically use break whenever you see other vehicles or turn right or left depending on the curve on the road. You reach your destination with ease avoiding any issues on the road. How could you do that?

You could do that because you are so proficient at driving that sometimes you don't have to be totally conscious and aware of what you are doing. And because you are so good at it, you can get from one place to another without even remembering how that happened. That's called subconscious competence.

If you want to be great at something you are currently good at, you have to do many repetitions. Do it consistently, don't stop until you become great at it, and when you do become great at it, do more. That will be your extra edge for self-mastery.

We find it is difficult to do exercises like squats and burpees in the beginning. Over time it gets easier with repetition. Whatever you want to do in life, you have to rep it out. You have to regularly keep doing it until your body becomes proficient at it.

If you pay close attention to what you are doing, you will find that you can actually create your own success story. What happens in the past is the past. What happens in the future is based on what decisions and actions you take today.

Have a coach or a mentor so that you can learn how to do what you want to do. No one has managed to solve all the problems on their own. All great leaders count on coaching; they take leverage rather than reinventing the wheel.

A coach can guide you, but you have to be ready to walk the path. To work on your skills, you should spend many hours repeating and practicing those skills.

Growth is a normal part of life. If you want to have massive growth, there's one thing that you're going to have to do; you're going to have to change! You cannot stay the same and get better results. It just doesn't work that way.

To be successful, you have to establish absolute clarity on where you are and where you are going, and then you have to get moving in that direction.

Repeat the actions that get you results and continue doing it.

3.9 THERE IS NO FAILURE, ONLY FEEDBACK.

At times, people come for coaching and tell me, "I failed in college", "I'm unsuccessful in relationships", "I started a business but had to close."

When we take actions to achieve our goals, and for some reason, they don't go according to our plans, we make a judgment that we are a failure.

Imagine you learned lessons from every incident of your life and didn't repeat the same mistakes; by now, you would have become the most learned and influential personality in your network.

Think about it.

What do you do when things don't work out as you want them to?

Do you give up and whine about how terrible life is, or do you pick yourself up and carry on?

Do you keep working to achieve your goals, or do you decide they must be unachievable because of the hurdles you face?

When you are at the cause side of the cause-effect equation, then anything that happens to you is good news. Even if it's a setback, you can learn from it and gain skills.

You may not have gotten the desired result now, that doesn't mean you will never get the result you want. Success is bound to be yours when you learn the lessons and conquer the gaps between what you have and what you want.

To be successful, you need to do things differently or consider that you'll eventually get the result you want and that your original time frame was just utilized to learn and practice.

Let's take a sales call as an example.

Clara made a presentation to the client for a large contract. The presentation went well, but she couldn't answer some difficult questions and failed to convince that client. As a result of this, she lost this order to her competitor.

She learned some vital lessons on answering tricky questions and how to convince clients to buy her products. She continued learning from all the rejections and groomed herself.

Today she is one of the best salespeople in the country, leading a large salesforce.

Every incident in life teaches us something. The best thing is, we should learn from the situations that other people are facing with an open mind.

I used to imagine how I would respond and deal with situations that other people faced if I were in their shoes from my younger days. Anytime I encounter a similar situation, I am better prepared to deal with it.

"Some of us learn from other people's mistakes, and the rest of us have to be other people." ~ Zig Ziglar

Let's also look at a situation-

Robin has a difficult manager. He smiles at him every morning without getting a response. He feels he has a bad relationship as he must have failed at something and didn't get the result the manager wanted.

Here, he doesn't have to think negatively. Instead, he can think: 'what can I do differently next time?'

'Do I have a clear vision of how I want my relationship with my manager to be?'

'Ah, that's right, I can suggest taking on that new project.'

As long as you are flexible in your actions, you will eventually get a different result, which maybe even better than the previous one. Learn from your failures to identify what you need in others to grow your abilities.

> *"Success is a lousy teacher. It seduces smart people into thinking they can't lose." ~ Bill Gates*

No failure is fatal, and what determines if the failure is fatal or not is the courage to continue with the lessons you learned from your flops.

Caution: Be careful of what you repeat. If you keep repeating a wrong move, you'll master it.

So, take every unsuccessful event as feedback. There is no failure because unsuccessful events teach you how to be successful next time.

Drill 3.7 – Steppingstones

Situations that didn't generate a favourable outcome.	Lessons Learned from Situations and how to apply.

3.10 HANDLING BOREDOM IN REPETITION

By now, you must have understood that repetition is the mother of learning and is vital to mastery. On the flip side, too much repetition may lead to boredom, wastage, and burnout.

Still, it's no surprise that for many people, the only way to survive a corporate job or a business that thrives on doing the same things over and over is to program their brains into thinking even the most tiresome of tasks as exciting.

In today's world of immediate gratification, a positive attitude is the main differentiator. Let me share what you can start doing to take the boredom out of repetitive tasks:

Setup Your Desk

Set your desk in such a way that your work is enjoyable and more manageable, not tiresome. Clear the clutter. The clutter can be negatively distracting and play a psychological role in making your task look messy and unorganized.

Place a photo of your family and loved ones on your desk. You can add a table lamp or anything that makes you smile, happy, and suits the place's decorum.

Stay Hydrated

When you repeatedly do the same process over and over and over again, it becomes easier to develop a killer headache or a migraine. By drinking water regularly, you would avoid dehydration and stay fresh.

Another helpful tip I use is having a glass of water rather than a bottle. Yes, a bottle is more comfortable. But by having to get up and get more water at intervals, you get the chance to stretch your legs. Use this opportunity to move and stay fresh.

Breaks

Take breaks when you can. It is essential to get 'on a roll' with your work, but breaking is key to staying fresh, so you do not make many mistakes.

When you take a break, engage in anything that makes you happy or laugh. Do anything that has nothing to do with what your task is.

Music/Podcasts

Music and podcasts are the ultimate solutions to avoid boredom. You should stockpile a selection of podcasts that tickle your fancy and are enjoyable. If you don't listen to podcasts, I would recommend you give it a go, especially if you regularly do somewhat monotonous jobs.

If you are more into listening to music, make different playlists that suit the task's requirements. If you want to make some difficult work light, make a playlist with uplifting songs. In our office, we play music to make the environment lively.

Learn to Enjoy It

Learn to enjoy your work for simple reasons because you chose to do it.

Believe that your work is valuable for the company, clients, and colleagues. Imagine the satisfaction your work can give to people.

Enjoy your work as it may give you a feeling that day moved fast. Once you get into a 'groove' and start making some decent progress, the hours slip by.

Treat your work like dance steps that you enjoy. Once you have your steps, it may make your work seem more productive.

A singer sings a song a thousand times but still enjoys it. The singer is the same, the song is the same, but the audiences are different. The secret of making repetition fun is to drive it for the audience. That is why the singers, during their live performances, engage their audience to create an experience for others and avoid boredom for themselves.

Drill 3.8 – Making Repetition Fun

List Your Repetitive Tasks	Variables That will Make it Fun

3.11 REPETITION AND THE SUBCONSCIOUS MIND

Repetition of thought makes 'thought habits' in the subconscious mind, which causes the mind to go right to work on an idea without one's conscious effort. The subconscious relates itself first with those feelings and thoughts that have become habits, especially if the thoughts have been passionately emotionalized by a deep and burning desire for their fulfilment.

Anyone can use creative imagination by employing the process of feeding his subconscious mind with definite desires. There is nothing to prevent anybody from applying this principle. However, you must realize that practical results are achieved only when you have gained discipline over the thought habits through the process of concentration of interest and desire.

Fleeting thoughts and mere wishes, which are about the extent of the average person's thinking, make no impression whatsoever on the subconscious mind.

Self-discipline begins with the mastery of one's thoughts. Without control over thoughts, there can be no control over deeds! Self-discipline inspires one to think first and act afterwards, but the common procedure that most people use is, act first and think afterwards.

Self-discipline gives one control over the emotions, enabling one to eradicate or suppress negative emotions and exercise positive emotions in whatever manner desired. One should understand that emotion rules the lives of most people.

Any leading idea, plan, or purpose held in mind through repetition of thought, will be taken over by the subconscious mind. If you want the mind to form a habit of acting on an idea, tell the mind what you want, over and over again.

The important thing about any statement is whether or not you believe it. If you tell yourself anything frequently enough, you'll get to where you will believe it.

The subconscious mind doesn't know the difference between right or wrong. It doesn't know the difference between positive or negative, and it sure doesn't know the difference between success and failure. It'll accept any statement that you keep repeating to it, through thoughts, or by words, or by any other means.

It's up to you to lay out your definite purpose, write it out so it can be understood, memorize it, and repeat it day in and day out until your subconscious mind picks it up and automatically acts upon it.

This process is going to take a little time. You can't expect to undo the negative thoughts that have been accumulating in your subconscious mind through the years, just overnight.

If you emotionalize any plan that you send over to your subconscious mind, repeat it in a state of enthusiasm, and back it up with a spirit of faith, the subconscious mind not only acts more quickly, but it also acts more definitely and more positively.

Use repetition to make these ideas yours. Don't just read these ideas once. Review this material repeatedly and emphasize their messages of thought & action through the power of repetition.

The more you work with Make a MARK in Life,
the more it will work for you.

3.12 BE THE MASTER OF YOUR GAME

Be Adaptable

Adaptability is the most crucial trait of successful people. With it, there is one thing that is sure to happen, that is change. Nothing is ever stable or constant. Successful people, successful relationships, and successful businesses are made up of people who have learned to be great at adapting to new circumstances and situations.

Focus

Focus, Focus, Focus. Prioritize and focus your efforts on what really matters and work at it until you become a master. To help with your focus, write your dream down plainly, and read it frequently. Simplify things and focus on what is essential and become great at it.

Passion

Relentlessly pursue love. Be passionate about what you desire to be excellent in. Without that, you won't go very far. The good news is that you can learn to love. Passion doesn't have to be happenstance. You can intentionally develop a passion for pretty much anything you want.

Power of Belief

Believe that you can. Everything is possible for the person who believes. Trust that your dream is necessary. Think about the posterity, about the potential lives you can change when you develop excellence in the area of your calling.

Believe that you must become excellent. Believe that you must achieve your dream, not only for yourself but for everyone who will be impacted by it now and in the future.

3.13 SPACED REPETITION TO ENHANCE LEARNING

Spaced repetition is revisiting information regularly at set intervals over time. The fundamental premise of spaced repetition is, the more often you encounter certain bits of information, the less often you'll need to refresh your memory of it.

A simple way to do spaced repetition is to use flashcards organized in a box or smart device. Set up a schedule for when you will revise the cards in each of the sections in your box.

If you answer a card correctly, you put it into a section that you will revisit less frequently in the future, whereas if you get the answer wrong, you move the card into a section scheduled for frequent visits.

Use Spaced Repetition for Effective Learning

Having a schedule is one thing, but then it's a matter of using it and retaining information. If a schedule is too complicated for you, this 4-step method is easy to get into and should yield similar results.

1. Review Your Notes

Within 20-24 hours of the initial intake of information, make sure the information is written down in notes and that you have reviewed them. During the reviewing session, you want to read them, but then look away and try to recall the most important points.

Remember, there is a difference between rereading and recalling, so be certain you look away and pull from your memories.

2. Recall the Information for the First Time

After a day of your first review, try to recall the information without using your notes. Try recalling while you're taking a walk or sitting down and relaxing.

You can also increase your efficiency by creating flashcards of the main ideas and quizzing yourself on the concepts.

3. Recall the Materials Again

After that, recall the material every 24-36 hours over the course of several days. They don't have to be lengthy recalls. Try a recall when you're standing in an elevator or waiting in line. You are still free to look at your notes or flashcards, but try recalling while working with those notes.

The idea of this step is to ask yourself questions and to quiz yourself in order to retain and recall this information.

4. Study It All Over Again

After several days, take out your material and study it all over again. If this information is for a test, make sure that this is done within a week before the test. This allows your brain to reprocess concepts.

Even without a schedule, spaced repetition feels natural and is way better than learning using the traditional methods. It expands on memory retention strategies like memory palaces too.

You can create memory palaces by storing different information at different physical places. Associate each location with something you want to remember. Whenever you want to recall that information, all you need is to visit your memory palace and pick up the information you stored.

Not only that, but this technique can be applied to all manner of things in life. Thanks to using flashcards and other methods, you can learn new languages, adequately prepare for tests, and much more.

Drill 3.9 – Spaced Repetition Exercise

Incorporate the things you want to learn and master in TOPS (The One Page Schedule – Refer to Fig. 3.1)

Please visit www.MARKModel.com/resources/ to download and print TOPS.

Explain your daily progress and weekly achievements to your accountability partner.

KNOWLEDGE

"Knowledge becomes your strength
when you act on it." ~ Rajiv Sharma

4.1 KNOWLEDGE AND THE KNOWLEDGE GRAPH

For the scholar Muhammad Tahir-ul-Qadri, knowledge was always grounded in the practical and the real. Even though it was all still profoundly spiritual, he believed a knowledgeable man was one who understood his situation and saw it as it truly was, without deluding himself or straying too far from the real world to the world of fantasy.

"If knowledge is not put into practice, it does not benefit one." - Muhammad Tahir-ul-Qadri.

Rita studied French through textbooks and also attended classes for some time. She eventually achieved her dream and went on a trip to Paris. Once there, she faced the prospect of speaking the language with native speakers in real-life situations.

She went to a café and tried to communicate with a waiter to order her lunch, but she was unable to decipher the waiter's French because of his accent. Rita recalled all the learning she went through, the words and verbs she had learned, but somehow in that situation, she could not understand the waiter. She realized that the learning she had done was all theoretical.

If you want to learn a new language in the real sense, there is an excellent way to do this – Spend time communicating with native speakers. Sitting in a classroom and studying verb conjugations will give you a sense of knowledge and accomplishment that satisfies your ego; however, you will fall short when it comes to the application. This is because speaking to people invites embarrassment, and one avoids such situations; therefore, is unable to achieve true mastery.

In the Knowledge section, we will further delve into the application idea. We have already explored the value of repeating actions over a period of time to achieve your goals and attain mastery in your chosen subject.

Dr Anders Ericsson, Professor of Psychology at Florida State University, researched many top performers in music and wrote a study in 1993 that an average of 10,000 hours of practice is required to reach the highest level. Later in 2008, Malcolm Gladwell supported 10,000 hours law in his book *Outliers: The Story of Success.*

When you work for 10,000 hours on a chosen subject, you could achieve mastery, where skill becomes your second nature and is absorbed into your subconscious mind.

I strongly recommend that when you start in any new field, guided practice is a must. Learn from those who are already applying or are going to use it.

When you make an error, there should be someone around to guide you and correct that mistake. Otherwise, you will practice errors and become a champion at it. Ten thousand hours is just the average benchmark. You may achieve mastery in less or may need more number of hours.

My mantra from MARK Model for you is:

Don't count your hours, repeat your craft with passion and precision. You are going to become better and superior at it.

Look carefully at the knowledge graph below. You can measure and plot your knowledge – the number of years of experience is on the X-axis, and the level of knowledge is on the Y-axis.

Examples of levels may vary from a functional level (associate) to a top-level (director). In each row, you can enter the levels of knowledge required for high-level performance in your field in the first column.

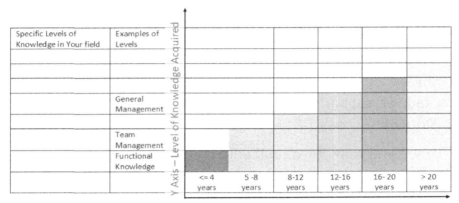

Specific Levels of Knowledge in Your field	Examples of Levels							
	General Management							
	Team Management							
	Functional Knowledge							
		<= 4 years	5 -8 years	8-12 years	12-16 years	16- 20 years	> 20 years	

X Axis – Years of Experience

Fig. 4.1

Knowledge is like a garden; if it is not cultivated,
it cannot be harvested.

Think about the number of years you have spent in your chosen field or career?

What's the level of knowledge that you have acquired within this time?

Mark yourself on the graph, considering your experience and knowledge level for an accurate assessment of your current situation.

This is the reality you will need to face frankly to harness your full potentials – only by facing up to your shortfalls will you be able to plot and assess the action that needs to be taken to improve.

Drill 4.1 – Five Years Forward Exercise

List the specific levels of knowledge required to achieve your goals. Prepare your future graph for the next five years. List your skills and be as specific as you can. For example, instead of saying Management Skills, be specific like, "Delegation Skills, or Building Trust in Teams." This is a practical resource that you can use and a basis for your learning journey for years to come.

Year	Knowledge/ Skills

4.2 DEVELOPING A LEARNING MINDSET

"Ever since I was a child, I have had this instinctive urge for expansion and growth. To me, the function and duty of a quality human being is the sincere and honest development of one's potential." - Bruce Lee.

When Bruce Lee spoke, people listened, ever wonder why that is? The above quote captures his philosophy, not just on self-discipline and a lifelong commitment to improving martial arts, but also the structure of what lay beneath; his approach to continually improving his knowledge.

No skills, no achievement, no fame can be achieved without a deep understanding of the Art of Learning. Here, we will explore this art in some detail to help you move to the next level and gain a systematic approach to learning that will serve you for many years.

Let us begin with understanding the Power of Learning. Again, let us reflect on Bruce Lee and consider a story from his life and contemplate the lessons.

Bruce Lee was an avid reader. To him, knowledge was the cornerstone of everything he believed in. His personal library contained more than 2,500 volumes of different works. It wasn't just martial arts that he was interested in; he regularly read about philosophy, filmmaking, boxing, and wrestling.

He was a student of the philosophy behind martial arts and even wrote the philosophical texts that he hoped would help his students understand how he lived his life. He brushed up on other contact sports to see what he could incorporate into his martial arts.

Though Bruce Lee lived an incredible life and was considered a masterful martial artist, he never stopped looking for opportunities to better himself. He felt that reading about the successes of those who came before him was an integral way to do so.

It's not the knowledge of only one field, but it's the combination of knowledge in various domains that puts you on the top of your game.

What underpins this story is Bruce Lee's mindset. He continued to learn, to take different elements from different facets of life and apply them to his one focus: martial arts. His mind was continually searching for new ideas, and this was part of his daily routine. There was no source of information he would not explore.

Reflect on this now in the context of your daily routine. You have created a learning plan for the next five years, now you must embed this plan into your daily routine (TOPS, Refer to Fig. 3.1), with a learning mindset that allows you to achieve your goals.

You need to practice your plan inside out. This implies that the learning process is a part of your mindset and part of your daily activities. You have got to live that plan with mindfulness and intention.

Think of people, things, and situations around you. There are experiences to be learned from everything in your environment. Nature is trying to teach you lessons.

To learn these, first, you must recognize the lessons and then understand how to apply them in your field.

Drill 4.2 – Mindful Learning

Complete the table below: Think about your environment, nation, community, role-models, and family. List the lessons you can apply in your domain/ field and build your knowledge base.

People/Situations I want to Learn from	Lessons I can pick from these people/ situations and how do I apply them.

Once you have listed your lessons and their applications, you will begin to see the world as not just a series of random events unfolding around you but a source of information. Your everyday experiences will not just pass you by - they will be lessons that contribute to your development and self-improvement goals.

The first step is becoming mindful of your environment and making this a daily habit, starting now.

4.3 KNOWLEDGE IS THE NEW CURRENCY

"The first principle is that you must not fool yourself, and you are the easiest person to fool." ~ Richard P Feynman

Self-delusion is the enemy of true learning and self-discovery. In the words of Nobel-prize-winning physicist Richard Feynman, you just have to be honest. Feynman was a true individualist – he pursued what he believed in above all else and cared not for others' opinions. In this way, motivation for him was always quite simple – he did what interested him with honesty and integrity.

Understanding your motivation is the key to recognizing your goals in a learning environment – building on your self-awareness is one way of achieving this.

Daniel was committed to becoming a lawyer. This was all he had thought about since he was a child. After getting into a law school, he found the studies difficult and uninteresting, but he persevered because he was hardworking. In his free time, he worked to help a local magazine – he would write creative pieces on photography and the growing influence of social media.

Daniel noticed that whenever he wrote, he felt himself come alive; it was magical to him. He felt connected to his work for the first time. After some reflection, he realized that his goal to become a lawyer was not his goal at all. It was a goal that his parents had set for him, and one that he had absorbed, but without real affection for it.

The goal was hollow - He didn't have the motivation to push through the difficulties because he didn't really want to become a lawyer.

Daniel then began his journey to change his life by moving towards becoming a creative writer. By doing so, he overcame any obstacle in this new field and achieved great financial success because he was genuinely committed to that path.

Many of us live our lives according to other people's ideas, sometimes without even knowing it. Real motivation cannot be forced, it must come from within, and that is a journey of self-discovery you must embark upon.

If you don't have the motivation to have a curious mind and a learning mindset, then the learning journey may not continue for long. It will be on and off. When you build a strong motivation, you will learn, but you will struggle if you don't.

People have varying motivation levels. For most people in the world, wealth is one of the strongest motivators to success. The easiest and fastest way to create wealth is through knowledge.

Now that you have created a learning plan for the next five years and are working to create a mindset to learn lessons from your environment with mindful intention, let's explore your motivation for learning in your chosen field.

"An investment in knowledge pays the best interest."

~ Benjamin Franklin

Drill 4.3 – Monetize Your Knowledge

How can you Monetize your existing knowledge?	
What knowledge in your field will be a real currency in the future?	

Your knowledge today is your income source for tomorrow.

Whenever you see a book from now on, start believing that it is not merely a stack of papers. Tell yourself, "This is a book that can provide me with the knowledge for earning more money. Imagine, a book of 200 pages is equal to 200 currency notes of $100 each."

Make sure to create an image of this in your mind if building wealth is your motivation.

You may lose your source of income. You may lose the wealth you have created so far, but you will never lose the knowledge you have acquired if you decide to implement that knowledge daily.

In his famous commencement speech to Stanford University, Steve Jobs talked about the time when he was fired from Apple, the company he had founded.

After a disagreement with the board of directors, he was asked to leave the company. He was lost for a while, but eventually, he decided to start a new company and begin all over again.

During this phase of his life, Steve Jobs created Pixar, the now world-renowned animation studio, and NeXT, a software company that was later taken over by Apple, leading him to regain his position as CEO in Apple.

The lesson from Jobs' Story? Although he had lost his status and his position, Jobs had the knowledge and the skills to start again and build his empire up from scratch. The knowledge he had built over the years was invaluable.

> *They can take away your job and title,*
> *but what they can't is your knowledge.*

With the implementation of the knowledge, skills, and a growth mindset, you will be able to create more wealth for yourself and your organization at great speed, as long as you apply the principles.

Drill 4.4 – The New Journey

List the skills that will help you rebuild your wealth if you start all over again today.

| |
| |
| |
| |

4.4 APPLY WHAT YOU KNOW

"Knowledge is not power. It is potential power." ~Tony Robbins

Not just knowledge, but the *execution* of knowledge is where the power lies. Knowledge is the source of those millions of dollars you have been imagining.

Every life lesson is crucial, and your implementation of knowledge is much more important.

"Knowledge is of no value unless you put it into practice."
~Anton Chekhov

Laura was looking to improve her knowledge of marketing strategies for growing her fashion accessories business. To improve her marketing knowledge, she read many books with marketing theories.

She attended courses that taught various approaches to marketing, filled her head with knowledge of these strategies, and became a marketing expert. However, her knowledge didn't translate into revenue, and business was going down.

She used her knowledge to grow her Instagram account to 10,000 followers, yet, that didn't get the sales she wanted. Her business model was for people to come to her store, while her followers were nationwide.

Whenever she put photos of her products on the Instagram page, it got many likes, and she realized that there was a demand for her products.

She began to reach people through direct messages and gave them options to buy online. She despatched the products to her customers through the logistics company. Customers started reviewing her products online, and gradually more than 50% of revenue was from online platforms.

Identify the learning that may not have given you financial benefits. We have all learned to feel knowledgeable with no real purpose but let us review these areas and face up to the fact that the learning was wasted because it was never applied. Knowledge is a tool that successful people use to accomplish tasks.

Review the knowledge you have acquired so far and imagine how you can apply them and turn them into monetary benefits.

Drill 4.5 – Knowledge Application

List areas where attained knowledge	What were your reasons to attain this knowledge?	What would you do to apply it for monetary benefits?

Be mindful of the practical result of your learning at all times. Even in areas where it is not apparent, try and find a practical use for the knowledge that will help you move towards your goals.

List the concepts/ topics you are reading/ learning.
What will you do to apply these in your areas of work?

By answering these questions, you can start to take purely conceptual ideas, and give them a practical grounding in your work. In this way, all knowledge will continue to be viewed in terms of the potential to enhance our work and eventually turn it into financial gains.

4.5 THE CULTURE OF KNOWLEDGE SHARING

"In learning, you will teach, and in teaching, you will learn."
~ Phil Collins.

A vital step in this knowledge journey is to create a learning family or a learning organization, where people learn from the mistakes of one another and take lessons not to repeat the same mistakes.

You, as a champion of knowledge, have to foster the culture of knowledge-sharing without fear. So, everyone shares their knowledge and lessons learned from their experiences to benefit each other.

Let us look at the story of John.

John was trained as a safety inspector – he had received mentorship and was doing the job well. In time, he was given a trainee to mentor. He started to teach in the same way that he had been taught, through lessons and detailed advice. But his trainee wasn't like him – he asked questions, was boisterous, and generally made John's life difficult.

At first, John was resistant to this, but ultimately, he got used to it. His resistance came from a fear of being made to look stupid. The trainee was smart and was asking questions that he could not answer. In turn, John had to learn new things to satisfy the trainee's curiosity actively.

Despite a rocky start to the relationship, the mentor ultimately learned much from the trainee's curiosity, and they both learned and benefitted from the relationship. Through being a teacher, the mentor, John was able to improve his approach to learning and become a better inspector.

Implementation of knowledge is not possible on a day to day basis if we don't build a culture of execution. That means everything we learn, we need to apply. Everything we know or learn; we need to teach others.

When you teach, you learn more quickly, so if you want to be a real master of something, pick up the topic, and start teaching others.

Drill 4.6 – Become a Teacher

List the concepts/ topics you are reading and learning.	How will you apply these in your field?	Write down the name(s) of people you will teach.

The value of teaching others is that it forces you to question your knowledge and to solidify ideas that you may not have understood completely. By explaining concepts to other people, you can identify the gaps in your knowledge and rectify them.

It is only through exploring these ideas that these gaps in your knowledge can become apparent.

Part of this is to have the courage to admit that you don't know everything. When you put your ego aside and make yourself vulnerable to being criticized, you become more invested in improving yourself.

Even something simple, like answering an IT issue on an internet forum, can lead to improvement. You want people to respond to your post and say it's beneficial. Even if they comment that you are inaccurate, this feedback will be helpful, and in turn, you will learn more carefully.

In this sense, teaching doesn't always have to be one-to-one mentorship. It can be anything that allows you to help others, which will, in turn, improve your knowledge in this culture of knowledge sharing.

4.6 THE POWER OF LEARNING, UNLEARNING AND RELEARNING

"There is no wealth like knowledge, no poverty like ignorance."
~ Buddha

Learning is of great importance because there are certain things, certain capabilities, specific skills that need to get upgraded with time, or they will inevitably fade. Without learning, we are all prone to stagnation.

For example, when an old version of an operating system becomes obsolete, we have to upgrade to the new version so that a computer will function properly.

In this fashion, we, too, can unlearn skills, clear out knowledge that is now obsolete, as well as look to continuously update our skills.

William was a successful print journalist. He started as a freelancer and was picked up by a large newspaper for his engaging work on human rights.

William's reputation grew in the industry, and he became very successful. He built up contacts and could always rely on getting his work printed in the largest newspapers, and through this, he always reached a large audience.

This was in the mid-90s. There was a lot of talk about the new technology that was going to change the world – the internet. He wrote this off as a fad and continued to receive great success and acclaim. Time passed, and more and more of the newspapers he wrote for started working online, and soon enough, their work was online only.

With some reluctance, William forced himself into working with computers and working online. He was thriving in this environment before long - he would research online, email his pitches, and his completed work, and he even started getting paid electronically.

William looked back with amusement on the days of his previous career, of using a notebook and a typewriter. It seemed archaic to think that he had worked in such a slow manner.

His reputation grew. But in time, people again started to talk about another new technology that was taking root in the industry. The readership of electronic newspapers was declining just as the print media had.

Suddenly everyone was talking about apps and social media sites. William was more adaptable to change now, and he didn't drag his heels like he had the first time. He saw the writing on the wall and moved quickly.

Instead of emailing his work to editors, he saw that the new technology meant he could directly reach his audience. He set up pages on Facebook in his name and created WhatsApp groups for business account. He created a website and linked all his media together.

Gradually, instead of dealing with large media houses who would publish his work, he would post by himself. He learned how a large online following got him a large audience – the traffic it sent to his website earned him money through advertising. Before long, people started asking him if they could write and post on his pages, and he was selecting others' work that he would post.

He reminisced of the days of email, and before that, typed articles, with amusement. He had gone from being a writer to an editor who curated other people's work. Had he ignored the new technology that was coming through, he would have been left behind. Instead, he moved with the times, learned new skills, and thrived in a new environment. Now and again, he sees newspapers fading away and marvels that no one within the organization had thought to make the changes and move with the times.

People are scared to change, scared to take chances, and, most of all, scared to fail.

Drill 4.7 – Review Your Skills

List the skills you need to unlearn, new skills you need to acquire, and existing skills you need to upgrade. This is important to ensure that you do not get left behind in your chosen area of expertise.

List of things I need to unlearn.	List of new things I need to acquire.	List of things I need to upgrade.
e.g. *the heavy accent of a particular region*	*e.g.* *a new language*	*e.g.* *improve pronunciation of certain words*

These ideas are tied to building mindful learning that we have already explored. You may have committed much of your life to build a reputation in a specific field, but you cannot rest on your past laurels.

If you don't continue to improve, you will start to stagnate. Even doctors must go to conferences to continually improve their knowledge of medicine in their chosen field.

Admitting this to yourself is a matter of being mindful and cultivating self-awareness. The people likely to stagnate and fail are those who believe they already know everything.

The same is true of 'unlearning.' Here, let us consider the idea of cognitive biases, which is where our mind fills in the blanks to a problem in a way that is not helpful or logical.

For example, the sunk-cost fallacy. A commonly cited bias is the idea that one should continue to 'throw good money after bad' in a situation.

Rather than pulling out of an investment or cutting one's losses, people are prone to continue down a bad path just because they have 'sunk' money into the problem, and they cannot accept that they will lose it. In doing so, they lose even more than they would have by walking away.

We want to use this idea of biases in mind to see things as they truly are.

Reflect on your past projects, whether they have any practical application today.

For example, the technology we used to take and develop photographs using negatives is no longer relevant today. We use our smartphones to take great pictures and create instant memories.

Unlearning is key to freeing up your mind to commit to the truly important things. If you have spent your life with passive projects, maybe now is the time to move on and work on the one that interests you.

You cannot learn everything in the world,
so, you need to make your choices.

4.7 NEW KNOWLEDGE TO NEW MINDSET

Learning is a lifelong pursuit and inevitably helps achieve personal, professional, and financial growth. As you have completed the exercises up to this point, you can better understand your relationship with knowledge.

The best news of all is that putting these things into practice consistently will help you improve further, leading to permanent change. It takes three weeks for the brain to recognize a habit and 3 months for new neuropathways to form in your brain to make that habit permanent.

When you combine and practice all the knowledge tips given in this book, you will be acquiring and creating new knowledge for yourself and the world. You'll become a great content generator, and this content is your experience.

"If you have the knowledge, let others light their candles in it."
~Margaret Fuller

Today if you look around, all the most successful people in the world, making the most wealth, are creators. That is the level you must aim for and achieve.

You can create new things by combining knowledge from different domains. When you join one component or feature with another component, you come up with something new.

Let's look at the creation of the smartphone. Telephones were already existing. They were combined with other devices like camera, music player, voice recorder, and computers to form the present-day smartphone.

Similarly, you may have knowledge of various domains; you can combine and connect the features of your knowledge to produce something new. With the execution of the new knowledge, you will discover many other possibilities and refine your creation.

The content you create will help you generate a new mindset. With a new mindset, you will begin the journey to the next higher level. This growth will become a continuous cycle.

Drill 4.8 – Generating a New Mindset

Look at the table below. Use it to summarize your knowledge and consider how it has allowed your mindset to change and grow. Think of the future and imagine how this cycle might continue as you move towards your goals.

New Knowledge that I have acquired by achieving mastery in a particular area.	My New Mindset that evolved because of my learnings and experiences.

Steve Jobs once spoke famously of trusting his intuition. His example was calligraphy. He studied this at college on a whim because it was beautiful and fascinating to him. He had dropped out of most of his classes because he couldn't see the value in them anymore; they seemed pointless.

He had studied calligraphy, thinking it wouldn't have any practical application, but when it came to designing the first Apple computers, it all came back to him. Apple computers were the first computers to have beautiful fonts, a significant move away from the tradition and ultimately a game-changer for all computers.

For Jobs, taking this chance and doing something different, in this case, a calligraphy class changed his mindset. Before, he dismissed a lot of knowledge as pointless, but when he was able to apply the calligraphy in this way, his mindset changed.

As he progressed with his life and career, he reflected more carefully on everything he had learned, which allowed him to progress to the next level of learning.

Like Jobs and many other accomplished leaders, you must trust that the knowledge you are learning will have a permanent impact on you and will change the future work you do for the better. Focus on the application of knowledge; how and where you will use what you are learning.

We all are born equal. We have almost the same reflexes, instincts, drives, needs, capacities, and rights; we all have the powers of perception, discrimination, attentiveness, retentiveness, reasoning, and so forth. Now it's up to you on how you want to use these capabilities.

The power lies in applying knowledge, evolving mindsets, taking consistent actions, creating habits, and acquiring new knowledge. Now you have the power to change your destiny by aligning to these four pillars of success.

Best wishes for your journey ahead.
You are bound to make a MARK.

If you need any help, get in touch with Rajiv Sharma for coaching on the MARK Model, creation of new knowledge and the use of existing knowledge in a new and creative way to generate new concepts, methodologies, and understandings.

Made in the USA
Monee, IL
30 December 2020